THE

GREAT

CONNECTION

ARNIE WARREN

Pallium Books
Fort Lauderdale, Florida

Published by:

Pallium Books

7027 West Broward Boulevard

Suite 272

Fort Lauderdale, Florida 33317 U.S.A.

Library of Congress Catalog Card Number: 96-92860
ISBN 0-9655148-4-6

Printed in the United States of America

10 9 8 7 6 5 4

To Ina Hathaway Warren who raised the bar for her son and grandchildren, Christopher and Leslie; to Robert Lefton, Ph.D. who brought insight to the second half of my life; and to a man in New Hampshire who makes this commoner strain to hear the sound of one hand clapping.

APPRECIATIONS

"THE GREAT CONNECTION should be required reading for all students about to enter the work force. It clearly shows the importance of knowing who you are and believing in yourself."

Richard B. Hayter, Ph.D., P.E.
Associate Dean of Engineering, Kansas State University

"You have caused me to focus on my own style and those of the clients with whom I deal each day. THE GREAT CONNECTION is must reading for anyone seeking to fine-tune people skills and maximize the development of sound business relationships."

Douglas S. Campbell, Senior Vice President, Investments,
Dean Witter Reynolds, Inc.

"I found the prose concise and the story simple and unpretentious. The message of 'know thyself' is consistent with today's management needs. The messages in THE GREAT CONNECTION are: 1) relevant, 2) discernible, 3) based on sound theory, and 4) clearly stated. Good Book!"

Lee A. Grutchfield, Ph.D., CEAP

"The style THE GREAT CONNECTION is written in is so engaging, so honest, so on target with things I have felt (and still do) that I can honestly say I learned more from reading your book than any I have read in years."

Rosita Perez, President, Creative Living Programs, Inc.

"THE GREAT CONNECTION is a welcome change to discovering personality styles. It should be required reading for everyone entering the work force. Imagine figuring out your boss or co-worker within days instead of years."

Victoria Northrup, Bombardier Motor Corp.of America

"THE GREAT CONNECTION triggers and defines explanations for your own successes and failures. Bob Hathaway's experiences will relate to many of your own. I recommend this for anyone who deals with people."

Hank Goldberg, sports commentator
WQAM / ESPN-TV

"THE GREAT CONNECTION is very perceptive. The communication skills you impart are in evidence throughout. This book should be retained as a road map by anyone who needs to relate—and that's a category that includes us all."

Steven Warm, Esquire

ACKNOWLEDGMENTS

There are many friends to thank for their help in writing THE GREAT CONNECTION. Terry Lubotsky, M.A., for planting the seed I write this story. Joan Warren who, with a single question, set me on this quest. Carolyn Stein who proved the universality of personal styles from Miami to Malaysia. Sheldon Weiss, Vice President / Partner, Media Plus, whose key suggestion made the story whole. Dick Bement, corporate consultant, who validated its acceptance in the corporate world. I am grateful to Richard Hayter, Ph.D., P.E., Associate Dean of Engineering, Kansas State University, who judged the content vital for graduate engineers entering the work force. Hank Goldberg, my favorite sports commentator, who made the time to read and offer candid comments. Marlene Naylor, M.Ed., for her suggestions and corrections. Caroline Mansur, Founder and Executive Director, Insight for the Blind, and Rita Ackrill who ferreted out the little words that needed polish. I thank Jerry Jenkins, The Jenkins Group, for his personal interest and guidance. Sid Levin, Vice President, Florida Power and Light, who felt THE GREAT CONNECTION delivered its powerful promise. I deeply appreciated the support of the late James McLamore. I am also indebted to Gayle Hansen, M.S.Ed., Corporate Training Director, for her structural comments. Margaret Carlson, M.S., P.D., Brenda Mayer, Joe Klock (caustic wit of Key Largo), and Ken Malden whose selfless interest and helpful comments did not go unnoticed. I am especially indebted to Jim Barber for his willingness to read and re-read and re-read and critique; for constantly being there as encourager, thoughtful listener, and creative jump-starter. And finally, my deepest thanks to Linda Sacha, M.Ed., Discovery Seminars, who gave me valuable counsel in shaping the language of each style, who challenged my dialogue every step of the way, and who gave me further insight into my own style.

FOREWORD

HIPPOCRATES FIRST RECORDED an astonishing revelation: no matter how many people inhabit the planet, each of us tend to fall into one of four behavioral styles. Obviously many nuances exist within each of the four styles, but the salient fact remains: under normal conditions, we exhibit the traits of one—our personal style.

But this alone, while personally satisfying, is not sufficient in today's interactional world. To improve your personal and business relationships is to know the styles of others to connect with them.

THE GREAT CONNECTION is the story of Bob Hathaway who learns how to connect with others . . . especially himself. You will find yourself in this book, too. You will discover who you are and what's holding you back. It will open the door for you to believe in yourself because—perhaps for the first time—you will know the person you are believing in.

THE

GREAT

CONNECTION

ONE

ONCE THERE WAS A LITTLE BOY SOPRANO desperate to grow whiskers. During his freshman and sophomore years in an all-boys school in Massachusetts, the other four hundred ninety-nine boys' voices had changed and their peach fuzz had stiffened. But Bobby Hathaway remained stuck on the cusp of puberty. He weighed seventy-nine pounds and stood four feet eleven inches tall. The boys constantly made fun of his high voice. "Hi, Bobby," they'd say pitching their voices as high as they could.

While Bobby could do nothing to accelerate his passage to manhood, he could do something to take away the sting of ridicule. He reasoned if everyone liked him they wouldn't make fun of him. And so this short, boy soprano decided to make sure every one liked and accepted him.

One morning, during summer vacation at home, he was lolling in bed when his mother entered the room. "Bobby Hathaway, time to rise and shine," she said, raising the window shade. He mumbled that she shouldn't do that; he was a slow, grouchy riser until he'd had his first cup of coffee. (It was something he'd heard a tough guy say in the movies.) His mother said, "Young man, give me one reason why you can't wake up cheerfully." She left the sunlit room and went downstairs to the kitchen. He thought about what she said. He couldn't come up with any reason why he shouldn't wake up cheerfully. Then it occurred to him that being cheerful was a trait others might appreciate. They'd like him for that. His own Mom validated it. So, he became life's little cheerleader.

When he finally passed through puberty, early in his Junior year, he was rewarded handsomely with a deep, bass voice. In addition to startling his peers with his authoritative tone, he had grown taller, and there was even a little stubble on his chin. So many changes. But his desire to make everyone 'like' him had not changed. It was indelibly instilled in him. If he saw someone down in the mouth he took it personally and felt an obligation to cheer them up; there was no reason not to. If he was involved in a confrontation he would quickly compromise; no offense, no rejection. He spoke enthusiastically using lots of superlatives. He was always, "Better than terrific!" Who wouldn't like to be around Mr. Sunshine? And so his formative years shaped the way he would always react to people and situations. He was driven to be accepted and approved of by others.

Thirteen years passed and the one-time boy soprano found a job perfectly suited to him: disc jockey in Miami, Florida. He had begun on the midnight to six shift. He was good at telling funny stories, and the people loved him. Within two years he was given the most important slot of the day: morning drive. And with his goal shaped by his formative years, he succeeded in getting a whole city to like him—for two decades! He made his living pleasing people.

KXOR in St. Louis, the nation's most listened to radio station, offered him a job. Now, 48, he was working for the jewel in the crown of the radio business. His three hour morning program consisted of one hour talking with listeners and telling stories and the remaining two hours interviewing people of celebrity status. He set out to win St. Louisans just as he had in Miami: enthusiastically, positively, cheerfully.

But his philosophy of winning listeners was too slow for his boss, A.J. Blaylock. His ratings were growing, but not fast enough. Bob was told he and the format would have to change!

Being hired by KXOR had thrilled him, but now the proposed change of format was so foreign and upsetting he almost wished he hadn't accepted the job. How would he confront the biggest challenge of his life?

TWO

$\mathbf{B}$OB LEFT THE RADIO STATION, walked down the hill, through the park, under the majestic St. Louis Arch, and sat on the steps of the levee by the Mississippi. In his hand was a memo from A. J. Blaylock, vice president and general manager of KXOR. For eight months Bob had been doing his radio show the way he'd done it back home, using the same format that brought him to the attention of Blaylock in the first place.

For the past couple of months, Blaylock sniped at him denigrating his cheery up-beat attitude. He made remarks like: "You can't be a good-time Charlie all your life."

Today's memo spelled it out.

K   X   O   R
The Voice of St. Louis

To: Bob Hathaway
From: A.J. Blaylock, Vice President & General Manager

Re: Format change

We pride ourselves at KXOR in 'owning' each time slot. Your ratings do not dominate the competition.

We are looking at a new format to increase market share. A show with real teeth!

Bob, I want you to be a controversial talk host. I am sure you will be willing to comply. At our meeting I'll lay out my plan.

A.J. Blaylock
AJB:le

He wanted Bob to be something he had never been before—a controversial radio personality.

Bob marveled that other talk hosts could engage in confrontation without a second thought. How come? Why such a difference in people? Was it the challenge of a new format he feared? No, accepting a challenge was something he loved doing. He'd done it when he first started in radio. He remembered an engineer commenting on a new wrinkle he was putting into his radio show saying, "Boy, you're really sticking your neck out on this one." And Bob had thought about that but felt good deep inside because he was taking a risk on himself. And when he succeeded, it was that much sweeter.

So, it was not the challenge of the new format that had him on the ropes. It was the controversial aspect of the format, and Bob feared confrontation. He didn't know which he dreaded more—a confrontation with his listeners or a confrontation with Blaylock. It was a lose-lose situation.

Bob reread the memo. '. . . be a controversial talk-host,' it said. Controversy was something he had avoided all his life. It pained him to think about the upcoming meeting, and, even more, it pained him to wonder why—ever since he was a little boy—he harbored this fear.

He didn't realize an elderly gentleman had taken a seat beside him. They nodded to each other and the old man gently said, "More than a few people come here to sort things out."

"I guess," Bob answered and extended his hand.

"My name is Bob Hathaway."

"Oh, you're the new broadcaster. I've heard of you." Shaking hands, he said, "My name is Crater. I'm a retired physician."

For a moment they watched the sun's rays dance on the powerful river and listened to the rise and fall of children's voices in the park.

"I guess working at KXOR is quite a plum," said the old doctor. "It must be satisfying to be at the top."

"As a matter of fact, it isn't."

"Oh? And why is that?"

Bob handed him Blaylock's memo. "Here. Look at this."

Dr. Crater read each paragraph of the memo carefully. "Very forceful person, this Blaylock. Isn't he?"

"I'll say. I feel like he's pulled the rug out from under me. He brought me from Miami to St. Louis because he liked what I did. Back in Miami, I was the number one personality. I worked twenty years to get there."

It was odd, but Bob felt Dr. Crater was someone he'd known for a long time. He talked freely about his past, but was completely unaware he was seeking the stranger's acceptance of him; that he was unconsciously persuading the stranger to like him. As they spoke, the old man nodded and smiled.

When Bob finished, Dr. Crater handed the memo back to him. Bob stuffed it in his shirt pocket, slouched down on the bench and folded his arms across his chest. They watched a tug boat guide a barge down the river. The stranger broke their silence.

"May I ask you a question?"

"Sure."

The old physician looked him straight in the eyes and asked, *Are you satisfied with yourself?*"

Bob took a deep breath and looked at the sun's glitter on the river as the question sank in; a question no one had asked him before. He closed his eyes, and muttered the question again. When he opened his eyes, the old man was gone. He turned and saw him walking through the park up the hill toward the street. Turning back to the river he repeated, "Am I *satisfied* with myself?" He knew the answer. It had been bottled up in him for as long as he could remember. He felt like screaming the answer. But instead, whispered to the river—"No."

THREE

THE NEXT DAY, Bob visited a new client, Mr. Fritz Hoffstetter. His business—Hams by Hoffstetter—was struggling to compete with the meat packing giants for space in the supermarkets. If anyone could persuade people to buy, it was Hathaway. Hathaway would generate excitement, and the supermarkets would *have* to stock Hoffstetter's smoked hams. Mr. Hoffstetter gave him a step by step tour of the process. Bob took notes during their meeting for commercial copy points. Upon leaving, Bob predicted business was going to be so great that soon Mr. Hoffstetter would be vacationing on the Riviera. Bob was exaggerating. It was his nature. He just wanted Mr. Hoffstetter to know that Bob Hathaway was an all right kind of guy.

Late the following afternoon, he went down to the levee. The old physician was there peeling a hard boiled egg. "Have a seat," he said as Bob approached. "Just having a little nourishment." He pulled a little packet of waxed paper from his pocket and opened it carefully. It contained salt. He first took a bite out of the egg, then sprinkled a little salt into the remainder.

Bob began. "I thought about what you said. You know, about being satisfied with myself."

"And are you?" the doctor responded returning the waxed paper packet to his pocket.

"No," Bob sighed.

"Then let me ask you another question. What is your biggest fear?"

"My biggest fear? What do you mean?"

"I'm not talking about fear of heights, or any of those phobias," he said.

Bob looked puzzled. "I'm still not sure what you mean."

"Well, let's start with your job. What's your biggest fear?"

"My fear that the ratings will go down."

"If the ratings go down, what would you conclude?" probed the doctor.

"That people didn't like me."

14

"What's your biggest fear within the radio station?"

"Fear of disappointing my peers."

"That would hurt, wouldn't it?"

"Of course," Bob said impatiently.

"Would they still like you?"

"How could they?"

"So what's your gut fear, Hathaway – on the air, off the air, everywhere you go – what's your gut fear?"

Bob answered slowly, "The fear of not being liked."

The doctor consumed the last of his egg then resumed with a more compassionate tone. "We all want to be liked, Bob, but in your case, it dominates your actions. It appears your very security and self-esteem depend on people *accepting* you."

"Doc, that fear question is amazing. When you ask yourself, 'What's my gut FEAR,' it cuts to the bone in a hurry, doesn't it?"

"Exactly. It cuts through defensive rationalization and exposes truth."

Bob looked off into the distance. A lifetime of scenes raced through his mind. Occasions when he responded to people – even strangers – to gain their acceptance.

Dr. Crater watched Bob come face to face with what—for years—had been deeply suppressed.

My biggest fear is not being accepted.

FOUR

THE DOCTOR BROKE the icy silence. "Have you ever been to the top of the Arch?"

"No, I haven't," said Bob absently. He was still stung by the chilling revelation that came from Dr. Crater's earlier question. Never in his life had a question about him been put so directly with the resulting answer so painful.

"Come with me." They stood and walked up the steps of the levee toward the Arch.

Riding up the Arch is not for people with claustrophobic tendencies. They squeezed into a little car, stopping along the ascent to switch to an even smaller car as the arch narrowed. At the top they entered a hallway with windows on either side.

"Stand over here," ordered the old man. "This

side looks east to Illinois."

"Wow!" said Bob. "Look how far you can see."

"And on this side," he said turning, "you can see west over Missouri."

Bob picked out the landmarks: the old court house, Union Station, the airport, the suburbs of St. Louis from Clayton to Chesterfield.

"Why did you want me to see this?" Bob asked.

"Come over to the east side again. Picture all the people living out there in Ohio, in Michigan, up to New England and down to Florida; everyone from here to the Atlantic Ocean. Now," he took Bob by the elbow and urged him to turn, "picture all the people in Missouri, Texas, Colorado, beyond to California and up to Alaska; from here to the Pacific. Imagine every single face of 250 million people looking up at you. Everyone is staring at you."

"And . . ."

"And not one person—of all those millions— cares what you choose to do in life. Not one!"

The doctor increased the pressure on Bob's elbow. "If no one cares what you *do* in life, Mister Hathaway, why on earth should you be spending your life seeking their *approval?*"

18

Both looked down at the city; the old man watching traffic move around the courthouse and out toward the airport, Bob not thinking about city traffic or even that he was at the top of the Arch. He was too overwhelmed by the power of the old man's statement. It was both stunning and accurate. *"No one cares what I choose to do in life, why should I spend my life seeking everyone's approval?"*

FIVE

THE LOGIC OF DR. CRATER'S series of questions was taking effect on Bob as they descended to the foot of the Arch. He reviewed the sequence.

I am not satisfied with myself because I'm not my own person. I'm not my own person because I'm always reacting to others and trying to be someone they would like. Consequently, I'm uncomfortable in offering an opinion or taking a position for fear of alienating someone. I've done this all my life because I feared people wouldn't accept me. But if no one really cares what I do in life, why am I driven to seek everyone's approval? *I am holding myself back!* Yet understanding this, intellectually accepting this, does not mean it's easily overcome. How can such a self-defeating pattern be changed?

"Doc, can we talk more over a cup of coffee at the hotel?"

The doctor smiled. "Sure," he said. The hotel was two blocks away.

As they walked up the hill to the sidewalk, Bob kept his pace slow so the old man would be comfortable. As they walked, Bob felt the baggage of his past lifting from him. It was an odd sensation.

They approached St. Louis' Old Cathedral and waited for the traffic light to change. As they stood there, Dr. Crater said, "Bob, do you know who your highest priority is?"

Another thunderbolt of a question, thought Bob. The light changed and they crossed the street. When they reached the sidewalk, Bob stopped, faced the doctor and answered, "God is!"

Dr. Crater reached out and put both hands on Bob's shoulders. "Look," he said softly, "if God gave you the gift of life, it is your responsibility to *do* something with your life to better serve your God, your country, your family, yourself. There's no way around it, son. *You have to be your highest priority.*"

SIX

As THEY ENTERED the hotel's coffee shop, another thought came to Bob.

They ordered coffee and the doctor asked the waitress if they had any Danish left over from breakfast. They did. He explained to Bob that his weakness was sweets.

Bob leaned over the table and said, "Doctor Crater you have asked me questions no one else in my life has asked, questions I never even thought to ask myself. I don't know why we met, but I want you to know how grateful I am for the time you're spending with me."

The doctor smiled. "Some things we don't try to figure out," he said.

Speaking softly, Bob asked, "Doctor, how do I break out of this mold that I'm in? This approval seeking drive of mine that's holding me back."

The waitress came with their order. Dr. Crater halved the pastry with his knife, opened a pad of soft butter and spread it on top of the Danish. "Bob, do you know who the founder of medicine was?"

"Hippocrates."

"That's right. Do you know what he observed?"

"I'm afraid I don't."

"He observed that people fall into one of four behavioral styles. One of four molds you might say. My purpose is to show you *your* personal style with its wealth of outstanding traits and get you to focus on them. Also, to show you traits that hold you back so you can neutralize and maybe even rid yourself of them."

"And this will help me break out of my mold?"

"It will help you know *who* you are and, most importantly, help you be *satisfied* with who you are." The doctor paused for a response. Receiving none, he enjoyed a bite of Danish.

Bob took a sip of coffee to offset the discomforting silence.

"Who are you?" asked the doctor breaking the silence.

"Who *am* I?"

"Yes. Give me a one word answer."

Bob heaved a sigh.

"Come, come," said the doctor impatiently, "who are you?"

"I'm a man."

"Who are you?"

"I'm a husband."

"Who are you?"

"I'm a father."

"Who are you."

"I'm a broadcaster."

"Who are you?"

"I'm a . . . I can't think of anything else. What are you getting at?"

"How old are you?" inquired the doctor.

"Forty eight."

"And in forty eight years all you know about yourself is what you've just told me?" Dr. Crater asked with some exasperation.

Bob stared into his half-filled coffee cup. He couldn't look the doctor in the eyes. "I don't know what you want me to say."

Dr. Crater looked across the coffee shop at the waitresses setting tables for dinner. Turning back to Bob he said, "Bob, do you know the secret to success?"

"Tell me," said Bob.

"The secret to success – no matter how you define success – is *total belief in yourself*. If you don't know who you are, how can you believe in that which you do not know? Only when you know yourself can you believe in yourself." Then he pushed his chair from the table, stood up, and said, "Go home, son, and make a list of your strengths and your weaknesses."

Bob went back to the radio station to get a legal pad. A.J. Blaylock was passing through the lobby as Bob walked out of the elevator.

"Oh, Bob," he said. "Come into my office."

The conversation was brief. He asked Bob to do a live broadcast of the annual "Veiled Prophet" parade: a somewhat Druidish St. Louis tradition honoring a prominent business man and the daughter of a civic-minded family. Since he had never seen the parade before, Bob told Blaylock someone else on the staff might be better suited; someone who knew the history of the event. He'd sacrifice his opportunity for the betterment of the radio station. Surely Blaylock would *like* him for that. The boss narrowed his eyes. Bob could see the muscles working in his jaw. Blaylock slapped the desk.

"All right. We'll get someone else."

Bob walked to the door feeling his common sense suggestion had pleased A.J. Surely the man would applaud his logic, admire his personal sacrifice, and approve of his candor. He thought, maybe I *can* get Blaylock to accept me after all. He couldn't have been more incorrect.

Blaylock shouted after him, "No guts, no glory, Hathaway!"

SEVEN

BOB COULDN'T SLEEP. Earlier in the evening, he'd called home and talked with his family in Miami. He told his wife what was happening at the radio station and how different Blaylock was since he first spoke with him eight months ago. When Bob accepted the job, the family decided to remain in Miami during Bob's first year in St. Louis just to be on the safe side. The family had been very excited for Bob because his talent had taken him to one of the great radio stations in the country.

Now, he lay awake thinking about Blaylock's sarcastic remark, the change of format, and the list Dr. Crater asked him to write. He got out of bed, padded down the stairs to the living room, and turned on the television. Charlie Rose was interviewing Betty Buckley, the Broadway star of CATS. Charlie asked what it was like getting ready to star on Broadway.

Betty said during rehearsals everyone told her where to stand, what to do, and how to interpret the songs; especially *Memories*. Her anxiety level became so intense it constricted her throat muscles preventing her from singing full voice. Opening night was only a few days away, and she was in a state of panic. What was it that was holding her voice back?

At three o'clock in the morning she was in her apartment crying uncontrollably out of fear, frustration and anger. Suddenly she said out loud, "But what about ME?" Then she told Charlie, "You can't express your true self trying to please others." The crisis was over.

Opening night, her interpretation of *Memories* stopped the show. Betty, in her moment of truth, knew who she was.

Bob turned off the TV and sat in the darkness thinking. *Who am I?*

He turned on the lamp, picked up his pad and pencil and listed his strengths and weaknesses.

EIGHT

It was noon on Friday. Bob felt particularly good after interviewing Dodger's Manager Tommy Lasorda and former first lady Rosalyn Carter. He and Katie, his secretary, were discussing next week's guest list. Monday: actress Liv Ullman and author Robert Olen Butler; Tuesday: movie stars Jane Powell and Jane Russell; Wednesday: Dr. Leo Buscaglia and a phone interview with Mel Tormé; Thursday: football great Rocky Blier and Leonard Slatkin, conductor of the St. Louis Symphony; Friday: comedian Louis Anderson and a phone interview with violinist Itzhak Perlman.

As he left Katie, he picked up his legal pad with the information Dr. Crater had requested. Bob headed for the arch where he saw the old physician standing by the levee. As he neared, the doctor turned and smiled. "I thought you'd be here today," he said. Together they walked along the levee till they reached an empty bench. He told the old man of the two people he'd just interviewed on the radio.

"You travel in high circles."

"Not really," he replied. "They pretend they know me; I pretend we're good buddies, but I'm not in their league. Who ever interviews an interviewer?"

"Hmmm," replied the doctor. "Let me see your list."

Bob handed him the pad. He had made two columns: strengths and weaknesses. They covered several pages. Some items included an explanatory note. For example, under strengths he recalled a time in his childhood when he sold Christmas cards to ninety-eight out of his ninety-nine paper route customers. And he was convinced he could have sold the ninety-ninth lady, too, if he hadn't had to stand two steps below her at the front door. *He was skilled in the art of persuasion.*

Under weaknesses he wrote of a time at a restaurant when he had ordered tea with his meal. The waitress brought coffee. He cheerfully told her he had ordered tea but that the coffee was okay. "Really, not that big a deal," he'd said. When the manager of the restaurant dropped by with the perfunctory "How was everything tonight?" he had replied that everything was perfect. A small item in the scheme of things, yet he could remember it twenty years later. *He resisted even the slightest confrontation to assure acceptance.*

The doctor read each column slowly. After he turned the last of Bob's pages, he looked out across the river gathering his thoughts for several moments. Then he took a pen from inside his jacket, turned to a fresh page on the pad, and made a chart of Bob's personal style. When he finished, he showed it to Bob.

"When you're on top of the world," he said pointing to the top half of the chart, "these are your most *effective traits*. But when you're dominated by the need for acceptance, you exhibit these *ineffective traits.*" He tapped the bottom of the pad as he handed it to him and watched his reaction to what he had written.

Bob was impressed. "I can't get over how you've pin-pointed everything so accurately," he said solemnly. "All my muddled thoughts about myself you've summarized so simply. Were you a psychiatrist, too?"

The old man chuckled. "No, just a doctor who has observed many patients in life just as

Hippocrates did two thousand years ago."

They were distracted by the *Star Spangled Banner* coming from Busch Stadium three blocks away.

"Oh," said Dr. Crater, "the Cardinals are playing the Dodgers today."

"Would you like to see the ball game, Doc?"

"Well, yes," said the doctor. "My goodness, I haven't seen the Cardinals play in a long time."

"Then let's go. You'll be my guest." Bob was pleased to treat Dr. Crater to the game because the old gentleman had taken such an interest in him.

Because of Bob's status with the radio station, they were given complimentary tickets to a private box overlooking first base.

"You get special treatment I see," said Dr. Crater.

"Comes with the territory," said Bob absently. His mind was on the traits Dr. Crater had listed on his chart.

They watched the game saying little to each other. Bob looked at his chart and went over each item.

He was pleased at his effective traits. Yes, he

was a *people person.* He could get along with anyone. As far as being *enthusiastic,* well, wasn't he life's cheerleader? He was *persuasive,* too. He'd proven that by the many products he'd sold over the radio. It was correct to say he was *optimistic.* He had always seen life positively ever since he was a little boy. It was also correct to say he was *entertaining.* He proved that in his job everyday.

A collective groan went up from the crowd.

"Oh, my," said Dr. Crater, "we're in trouble."

Bob looked up. The Cards had walked a Dodger. Their 2-1 lead was in jeopardy. The next batter slammed it over the wall, and just like that the Dodgers were leading 3-2. A relief pitcher was summoned, and Bob turned his attention to the second half of his chart with some discomfort.

The first item on the ineffective traits list was: *avoids confrontation to maintain acceptance.* True, he thought—if I confront, I risk rejection. This was his major ineffective trait. He stared at those words and wondered how on earth Dr. Crater could help him get over this, the very root of his present problem.

He moved on to the next ineffective trait:

exaggerates. I do make things appear better than they are. But I do that to keep people up, he figured. He moved his finger down the chart to *overly enthusiastic.* He wondered why that was an ineffective trait. He decided it was because he got too carried away with the momentum of the moment.

Talks too much was next on the list. He rolled his eyes and remembered how many times he'd come home from a meeting and said, "Gosh, I talked all evening. I couldn't shut up!" Why do I do that? he asked himself. What am I trying to prove? Then Bob realized he kept talking to prove he was worthy of being accepted, and he nodded his head in resignation.

Difficulty staying focused was last on the list and with chagrin he agreed.

He leaned over to the doctor. "Doc?" he asked, slapping the paper with the back of his hand, "Do others know all this about me?"

"Yes and no," he answered frankly. "They know you exaggerate and tend to talk too much, but they don't know *why* you do that. They accept you because you are fun to be with, but I think in many instances they don't take you seriously."

Bob told the doctor he had to go to the men's

room. He really just wanted to be alone. Gone was the mild euphoria of a few days ago. Focusing on his negatives was depressing. He reflected that maybe his years of migraine headaches were a manifestation of this internal struggle. Dr. Crater's probing had brought it out in the open. He thought, I not only have to confront Blaylock, but also myself!

Fifteen minutes had passed, and Dr. Crater had come to look for him. He found him leaning against a wall staring at the cement floor.

"Are you all right?" the doctor asked.

"Fine," he replied not looking up.

"No, you're not," said Dr. Crater. "Want to talk about it?"

"Doc," he began, "I know you're trying to be helpful, but this is just depressing me. How can I stop being what I am? How can anyone stop being what they are?"

"Come on back to the box," he said taking Bob's arm, "it's more private."

Settling in their box seats, Doctor Crater said, "Bob, you don't stop being who you are. It's not a case of changing Bob Hathaway into someone he's not."

"Doc, maybe I'm too old for this?"

38

"As far as age is concerned, I think, for many reasons, the older you are the better. With some years behind you, you have a better perspective of yourself and your style. Don't you see what this knowledge can do for you? For the first time in your life your ineffective traits have been identified. Lift that baggage, neutralize it, throw it away, and focus on your God-given strengths."

"And this will help me with my job?"

"Son, this will help you with your *life*."

Pendleton powered one over the right field fence, and the Cardinals hung on to win 4-3.

Driving home, Bob was amazed at how much had come from the simple question: "Are you satisfied with yourself?" How that led to determining what his biggest fear was. And at the top of the Arch, Doc saying that no one cares what you do in life, so why try to please everyone? Then, by the cathedral, Doc telling Bob that he alone was his highest priority. And finally, the chart itself that Doc had written for him. Now, the big question was: How will this help him deal with Blaylock?

Bob approached Webster Groves, the St. Louis suburb, where he rented. It was a beautiful town of old homes purchased by people who loved the quaint and historic setting. As he drove to his home, he wished his wife and two children could be here to share this.

He counted his blessings. He had a lovely wife and children. He was at the top of his craft and making good money at KXOR. His large audience appreciated him. He appeared to have it all. Many would gladly change places with him.

His agony over confrontation and his dread of not being accepted were painfully real. Yet, no matter how successful we perceive people to be, he mused, there is a hidden, maybe even suppressed, darker side. Does everyone have demons inside we try to deny?

Pulling up to his house, he saw the neighbor's dog sniffing at the trunk of the maple tree in the front lawn. He parked the car and thought of *his* dog back home: a golden retriever. He recalled, when he bought the pup, the breeder saying, 'They're the easiest to train *because they want to please so much.*'

"Good Lord," said Bob, "I'm just like a golden retriever." As he stepped out of the car he said, "If I'm a golden retriever, then Blaylock is a pit bull."

NINE

IT WAS MONDAY. Bob had just said good-bye to his guest Robert Olen Butler. He sat back in his broadcast chair and read the inscription Butler had penned in the front of his book, *On Distant Ground.*

> *St. Louis*
> *March 5th*

Dear Bob . . .

> *Thanks for a sensitive and intelligent interview—my very best ever.*

> *God bless you!*
> *Robert Olen Butler*

A wave of pleasure and satisfaction came over him, but it was short lived. Lorna, Mr. Blaylock's secretary, entered the studio to tell him A.J. and the program director wanted to discuss his show. They were waiting for him. Bob closed Butler's book and headed down the hall to Blaylock's office.

"Hathaway needs a new format to make the ratings pop!" the boss began. "Something that's controversial. And if you guys can't come up with anything, I will."

The program director spoke. "I see Hathaway opening with a monologue, laying out one or two issues with plenty of personal bias, and then taking to the phones. Be the devil's advocate with every caller. Even the callers who agree with you, make them prove their point. If they don't? Nail 'em! People will stay tuned because each call is a battle of wits."

The boss looked Hathaway dead in the eyes, "I like it, what do you think?"

Bob had not worn a jacket into the meeting, and wetness was spreading in the armpits of his shirt. He envisioned irate callers laying him out in spades—ready to run him out of town—for his position on an issue. He was afraid he wouldn't be able to intellectually recover, let alone emotionally recover.

"May I think about this?"

"I'll give you till Friday," said Blaylock. "Let's meet at 7:30 a.m. and get this settled." He leaned across his desk, pointed a finger at Bob, and said through clenched teeth, "I want you to shake up this town!"

Bob left hurriedly. He didn't go upstairs but called Katie from the lobby telling her he wouldn't be back today. Then he headed out to the levee. He rushed across the park, under the Arch, down the steps and looked both ways quickly for the old doctor. Bob didn't see him. He looked again more carefully. The doctor was not in.

TEN

HE WAS ANGRY, frustrated, scared. How do you change a golden retriever into a pit bull in a week, he wondered. Should he run to a lesser radio station and keep doing what he was good at? Or should he stay and risk embarrassment, maybe even risk being fired? Oh, where was the doctor? He needed to talk to him urgently. He needed advice, counsel, and support!

Approaching him quickly, a man, fortyish, asked, "Are you Mr. Hathaway?"

"Yes, I am."

"I have a message from my father, Doctor Crater. He told me to tell you he's at Barnes Hospital."

"Hospital! Doctor Crater is in the hospital? Is he all right?"

"He's resting comfortably."

"But what happened!" Bob almost shouted at the son.

"He fell on the sidewalk at his home and broke his wrist."

"But why is he still in the hospital?" Bob asked.

"He fell because he fainted. Anyway, I have to get to class. I'm an engineering professor at the University of Missouri. Dad wanted me to let you know where he was. I'm really late. Talk to you later." He climbed the levee steps two at a time. When he reached the top he turned and shouted back, "By the way, my name is Josh. We'll talk sometime. Tell Dad I'll see him tonight."

ELEVEN

Bob DROVE TO BARNES HOSPITAL, parked, and hurried to the information desk in the lobby. "What room is Doctor Crater in please?" he asked the receptionist. She picked up a clipboard and ran her finger down the page. "You said Crater?"

"Yes."

"He's in room 323."

"Thank you," said Bob as he headed for the elevator.

The door of 323 was slightly ajar. He nudged it open, and there was Dr. Crater lying in bed with his right hand and forearm in a cast. Some wires from his chest were connected to a monitor on a shelf behind his bed. His heart beats were being recorded.

"Doc, what did you *do*?" asked Bob.

"Ah, just old man stuff. Good of you to come, Bob, pull up a chair." He spoke evenly and quietly. He looked frail in the hospital bed; all white, except for his soft blue eyes. The doctor pushed a button to raise the bed slightly. What kindness was in those eyes thought Bob as he sat by the side of the bed. "Are you going to tell me what happened?"

"I was sitting on my porch steps and stood up too quickly. Simple as that."

"But these wires to your heart?" pressed Bob.

"Let's just say I'm under observation." He quickly changed the subject. "Now, how are things going at the radio station?"

"They've given me 'til Friday to come up with a controversial format."

"How controversial?"

"They want me to mix it up with the callers."

"And how do you feel about it?"

"Terrible. I don't want to do it. Haven't I been successful *without* doing that? Why should I risk alienating half the audience?"

The doctor didn't answer. He just looked at Bob expectantly. Bob continued.

"I'm struggling with what you said when we were at the Arch; when you said no one cares what I do in life so why seek their approval. It's so hard to put that into practice. What my mind accepts, my life-long habits fight. Why would I want to put myself through this? If I could get over this fear of not having everyone's approval, I could do it. You call conquering this fear growth. I call it torture."

"Bob would you pour me a glass of water from that pitcher please?" he asked raising his head from the pillow.

Bob rose, poured the water into a tumbler, took a straw, flexed it, and brought it to the doctor's lips.

"I met your son, Josh. He wanted you to know he'd drop by this evening."

"I'm glad you met him, and thank you for the message." He took another sip of water and lay back down. "Bob, since we met, I've asked you a lot of personal questions. I believe you have taken them very seriously. Am I right?"

"Yes," said Bob.

"When you said to me, 'How do I break the mold,' I knew you were ready to learn and to grow."

"That's right," said Bob.

"Mold is another word for your individual

style. How you relate to the world. *You* are driven to please people. I don't know what the origin is, but I suspect it was something in your childhood that took hold and never left you. It's become an obstacle preventing you from using your most effective traits. It's like taking a car on a trip and having one foot on the brake all the way for fear the car won't stop if you need it to. You never get anywhere with the brakes on."

Bob interrupted, "Doc, when I bought my golden retriever the woman said, 'They learn quickly because they want to please so much,' and I thought I was like that."

The doctor smiled and started to continue, but Bob kept on. "Then I thought that Blaylock was like a pit bull."

"Good," said the doctor smiling. "It's not a very scientific way of putting it, but you've identified two of the personal styles. Do you know what your style is called?"

Bob shook his head. "No."

"Influence."

"Influence?"

"Correct. That means you are a gifted people-person. That can work for you or against you. If you get up each morning with a missionary's zeal to work with people and listen to people and not be afraid to confront people, then you will operate from a platform of power. If, however, you seek to gain people's acceptance by pleasing them you will never be true to yourself, or them for that matter, and you will never know what it means to be *you*."

The doctor's voice was lower. He was tiring. Bob offered him more water. Dr. Crater drank, lay back on his pillow and pressed the button to lower the angle of his bed. Then he carefully turned on his side with the cast forcing his arm to jut pointedly at Bob.

"Bob, it's time to grow up. It's time to stop living *your* life to suit others. It's time to focus on your very special effective traits. It's time to be your own man!"

The doctor paused for a moment.

"We have three days before your Friday dead-line. Come back tomorrow and we'll make a chart of Blaylock's style. By Thursday you'll have heard about all four styles. And with that under-standing, you'll be able to deal with anyone . . . comfortably."

The doctor eased back on the pillow, his right arm across his waist, his left hand clutching the sheet at his neck, his eyes closed.

Bob leaned forward and whispered, *"Effective traits are potent; ineffective traits are impotent."*

A smile fell across the doctor's face. "That's very good!" His left hand relaxed on the sheet. He was asleep.

TWELVE

BOB ARRIVED HOME around four o'clock in the afternoon. He couldn't stop anticipating Friday's meeting. This was no ordinary meeting, this meeting would change his life for better or worse. He felt like taking a nap before supper—a brief escape—but instead picked up the phone and called his good friend and accountant, Tom Wilcox. Tom knew Bob well and had advised him not only on financial matters but personal matters as well.

He was lucky. Tom was available. Bob told him of the imminent change in format; how he doubted he could handle it or even *want* to handle it. Should he hang in for the money or bail out now before the format change? Did Tom have any suggestions? What was his advice?

Tom asked many questions. When did his contract expire? What was the lease arrangement where he was living? How much furniture had he bought? How much money had he saved? How well versed was he with the local and national topics on the minds of St. Louisans? What would he do if a caller was more articulate than he was on a given subject? If they fired him, what would he receive in severance? Could he get another job if they fired him? Did he still want to stay in radio? Did he enjoy the show he was doing? Were the ratings going up or down?

They talked for nearly an hour. Tom let nothing slip through the cracks. No detail was too small for Tom to address. He ended telling Bob he'd get back to him Wednesday.

"Wednesday! Tom, I need your input now!"

"I have to think it through," Tom cautioned. "You have till Friday. Let's not be impulsive."

"But, Tom," he protested, "what do *you* think I should do? What does your gut say?"

"Bob, I need time to think about it." And with that the conversation ended.

THIRTEEN

THE NEXT DAY, Tuesday, Bob entered the studio with his notes for the day's guests: Jane Powell and Jane Russell. Jane Powell was promoting a line of petite size clothes for women. Jane Russell was promoting her book, *My Paths and Detours*. As he placed his notes before the microphone, he saw a handwritten memo from A.J. Blaylock. "See Me."

"Damn," fumed Bob, "now what does Blaylock want?"

He had been in a cheerful state of mind looking forward to interviewing the two Janes. He'd grown up watching the Technicolor® musicals with Jane Powell. He liked her singing voice. And as for Jane Russell? Well, who could forget *The Outlaw*; a 1943 movie that was, for the times, hot

55

stuff. He went down the hall to Blaylock's office.

"Go right in," said Lorna.

"Have a seat, Bob," said Blaylock not looking up from writing a note in the folder before him.

A cold blue-gray carpet dominated A.J.'s office. Austere mahogany bookcases filled with pricey glass sculptures stood surrounded by a wide window expanse draped in damask. A.J.'s desk was a beautiful beveled glass top with a small Waterford clock guarding one corner. No drawers. A single folder lay open before him exposing a small sheet of paper. His notes reflected the date, time of day, a brief two sentence summary of the prior meeting, and a sentence to indicate the follow-up action to be taken. He was a man of amazing brevity and discipline.

"Now then," Blaylock said looking up at Bob.

"How are you this morning?" began Bob testing the boss's mood.

"Fine. Fine," he answered sharply. "What do you have on the new format?"

"To tell you the truth, I'm still mulling over the program director's suggestion. Take a topic or topics, do a monologue, ask for phone calls, and play the devil's advocate with the caller." Bob remembered Dr. Crater's admonition that he was apt to talk too much, so he stopped there.

"Haven't you done any more than that?" A.J. shot back.

A red flag went up in Bob's mind. A confrontation was brewing. He could feel his heart beating. He became confused and wanted to escape.

"Well?" asked the boss.

"You told me we'd finalize this on Friday," he said nervously. "Friday I'll have all the details." He rose from his chair, grabbed it from behind and pushed it to its position near the desk.

A.J. glared at him. Bob kind of half-smiled hoping Blaylock would reciprocate. He didn't. "Fine," he said slamming shut the folder, and Bob walked back to the studio.

Jane Powell was a delight. She was a bubbly person in love with life and in love with love. And when she left, she gave Bob a kiss on the cheek. He would remember that kiss every time he saw one of her old movies on TV.

The news had concluded at the top of the hour, and Bob's mike was opened. He began by giving a brief background of his next guest: Jane Russell. "Ms. Russell," he asked, "in your book you mention a beautiful childhood scene where you and your grandmother sat by the trunk of an oak tree on her farm. What did you talk about?"

Jane told how her grandmother read Bible stories to her. Her grandmother made the stories come alive and she always explained the message behind the stories. This gave Jane a path to follow, and when she followed that path, life was good. When she detoured from that path, things went sour. That's why she titled her autobiography *My Paths and Detours*. After the interview she gave Bob a hug.

Bob had a brief meeting with Katie to confirm Wednesday's guests: Mel Tormé by telephone and Dr. Leo Buscaglia in the studio. Then he left to see Dr. Crater.

On the way to the hospital, he thought about Jane Russell's book title. He wondered if his coming to St. Louis was a path to the good life, or just a sorrowful detour.

FOURTEEN

Bob NUDGED THE DOOR open to room 323. The blinds at the window were turned to deflect the sun's glare. The bed was raised and Dr. Crater was resting with his cheek against the pillow facing the door. His eyes were closed.

"Doctor Crater," Bob whispered. "Are you awake?"

The doctor opened his eyes and smiled. "Just resting my eyes," he said. "Good interviews this morning. I really enjoyed them. You do good work, Bob."

"Well, they were easy people to talk with. They both had stories to tell. I hope the audience liked it. How are you feeling?" There was concern in Bob's voice.

"Oh, they have me on some heart medicine.

Keeps me calm and even. I feel like I'm in slow motion."

"Why the heart medicine? I thought you were here for your broken wrist?"

"They discovered a slight arrhythmia, so I take one pill to keep my heart beat from going too slow and another to keep it from going too fast. But enough of me. What is happening with you?" He groped for the light switch behind his pillow, found it, and clicked it on.

Dr. Crater looked paler than Bob had remembered seeing him yesterday. He hadn't shaved, and his hair needed combing. It was the first time Bob realized the seriousness of Dr. Crater's illness.

"Doc, maybe I shouldn't be bothering you right now. Wouldn't you rather rest?"

"Lord, no," he said with some energy. "All I do here is rest. Talking about your problem is good for me; takes me out of myself. So talk, son, what's going on?"

"I called Tom, my accountant, last night."

"And?"

"And we talked for an hour."

"Why did you call *him*?" asked the doctor.

"Get his opinion on whether to do what

Blaylock wants or . . . quit."

Doc Crater glared at him. "Did you say quit?"

"Yes," said Bob sheepishly looking up at the ceiling.

"Go look at your style again," sighed the doctor, "and ask yourself why you're thinking of quitting."

"You think it's because I fear confronting Blaylock. Right?"

"Confrontation is a major fear of yours isn't it? Escaping confrontation is what you've done in the past, isn't it?"

"Yes, you're right," Bob answered slowly, "but I just want to cover all my bases. I'm still working it out, Doc."

"Oh," said Dr. Crater raising his eyebrows and nodding. "And?"

"And Blaylock is on my case. Called me in this morning to ask why I hadn't come up with any format details yet. The guy thrives on controversy—on the air and off."

"Well, I think it's time you learned what Mr. Blaylock is all about."

"How will understanding him help me?"

"You'll see," said Dr. Crater as he pushed the button to raise himself straighter in the bed. "Tell

61

me about him. Start with what his office looks like."

Bob began with the desk, and how he used a single file folder with a small piece of paper for his notes. His chair was raised higher than the chairs on the other side of the desk. His wall had pictures of him with important people. His bookcases displayed valuable glass sculptures. His clothes, tailored. Shirts, French cuffed. Fingernails, manicured. He used his height, about 6'2", to intimidate. He'd stand close to you, forcing you to look up at him uncomfortably. He referred to his letters of recommendation as "pedigrees." Bob recalled a meeting when an announcer had made a suggestion Blaylock didn't agree with. He belittled the man in front of his peers. On the other hand, if someone came up with an idea he liked, he would implement it and take the credit. Bob stopped. Only the hum of the heart monitor was heard.

Doctor Crater asked, "Do you have your legal pad with you?" Bob nodded and retrieved it from his briefcase. "Now if you would, Bob, scoot that eating table over so I can write on it."

Bob wheeled the table into position and adjusted the height so it was easy for Doc to write on the surface. The doctor drew a chart with his left hand—not without some difficulty—just like the one he had drawn for Bob.

Blaylock's Style

Effective Traits
- Direct and Self-Assured
- Seizes Challenges
- Competitive
- Results Oriented
- Fearless in Confrontation

Ineffective Traits
- Boastful
- Dictatorial
- Blunt
- Argumentative
- Difficult Listener

"Bingo," said Bob. "What do you call his style?"

"Dominance."

Bob burst out laughing. "Dominance? How about Dictator!"

"Ahh, that's because you've only seen one side of his style. You think of him as a dictator

63

because he stresses his *in*effective traits with you. To deal with him you must be direct, to the point. To survive with him, you must not allow your feelings to interfere with the relationship or his decision making process."

"In other words," said Bob, "he doesn't consider how I feel about changing into a controversial talk host?"

"Blaylock doesn't consider it because you haven't brought it up. The bottom line for him is higher ratings, which translates into more sales and more money for the station. That's his job; his responsibility. He expects you to be as direct in your answers as he is with his questions. It's too bad he goes about it the way he does."

"So, where does that leave me?" asked Bob.

"Where do you want to be?"

Oh great, thought Bob, yet another philosophical question. He poured some water and gave the doctor a sip. Dr. Crater thanked him and relaxed into his pillow.

"Bob, what have you learned about personal styles?"

"That one is called Dominance and the other Influence and they both have effective and ineffective traits."

"And?"

"And we're different."

Dr. Crater was becoming frustrated. "Can you see any advantage to *knowing* the differences?"

Bob looked off thoughtfully.

"Bob, suppose you were a car salesman and a man like Blaylock came in to buy a car. After you listened to him for a while, you'd realize he was displaying the personal style on that chart I drew for you. Here's how you'd know. He'd speak directly, wouldn't he? He wouldn't waste time. He'd probably be abrupt, maybe even appear rude, just to let you know *he* was calling the shots, not you. And if you tried to *sell* him, he'd put you in your place. How would you deal with him?"

"I'd act like Joe Friday, just the facts. I wouldn't waste words. I'd figure he was an impatient person who knew what he wanted."

"Right. Now, how would you make sure you'd get this man with the Dominance style—the same style as Blaylock—to buy the car?"

"That's easy. I'd talk to him the way he wanted to be talked to."

Suddenly, Bob's eyes popped wide open. The light bulb went on. "Ah-*hah*! *Now* I see what you're getting at. By knowing the other person's style, you can talk more effectively."

"You've got it. *You've got it!*"

"And while you're busy adapting to them, your own insecurities take a back seat."

"Son, you've just discovered the treasure." The doctor was *very* happy.

"So I should adapt to Blaylock's style at the Friday meeting?"

"Of course. Do you think that he—for one second—is concerned about your feelings? Blaylock sees you only as a vehicle to get higher ratings. It's likely he'd respect you for standing up to him. Knowing that, doesn't it make it easier for you to confront him? Doesn't it make it easier to throw your sensitivities out the window?"

"Fighting fire with fire, right?" said Bob.

"I prefer the word you used before: *adapt*. Adapt is a good word. Being able to adapt to various personal styles is a quality all masters of people skills have."

They both took a respite.

Bob looked at Doctor Crater who had settled back into his pillow and closed his eyes. "Your lessons are taking hold, Doc," Bob said smiling.

"Let's not talk anymore. I need to rest. Come

and see me tomorrow afternoon. We've still two more styles to discuss. Then you'll have the complete blueprint. I don't mean to be rude, but I *am* tired. Please close the door when you leave."

FIFTEEN

DR. LEO BUSCAGLIA hustled down the hall and into Bob Hathaway's studio. Bob stood up to shake his hand, but Dr. Buscaglia already had his arms wide open to give him a hug. (He believes everyone needs four hugs a day.) Buscaglia was a wonderful, energetic guest.

During the first commercial break, Dr. Buscaglia leaned across the table and said, "You really *listen!*" It was strictly a broadcasting skill, but a skill Bob would later come to value in his everyday life.

After the interview, Bob's secretary came into the studio. Usually Katie waited upstairs in her office, but not today. Bob thought her purpose was a hug from Leo. That was partly correct. Her main purpose was to alert him that a newspaper reporter had called asking about the new format starting Monday.

So, Blaylock had leaked it to the press. He wasn't waiting for Bob's ideas on a new format. Bob had no choice in the matter. Friday's meeting was a mere formality. Bob left the building immediately, drove home, and called Tom.

Tom outlined in detail Bob's financial position. What his contractual penalties would be if he left the station. What his lease penalties would be and the cost of moving if he left town. He determined how long Bob could live on the money he'd saved. Then he itemized how much Bob could save if he stayed for the remainder of his contract. He gave Bob a true financial picture from which to make a decision.

"Tom," said Bob, "you've known me for a long time. Forget the dollars and cents for a moment. What do you think I should do?"

"You have the facts, Bob. Now, follow your heart, my friend. Follow your heart."

SIXTEEN

BOB LEFT HIS HOME in Webster Groves and drove over to the hospital. As he entered Dr. Crater's room, he met the nurse coming out. She took him by the arm back into the hall.

"Please don't stay too long. He didn't have a good night," she said.

"What's his condition?" he asked.

"It's his heart," she said. "I can't really tell you any more than that."

"I'll be brief," he promised and walked into the room.

Dr. Crater had an IV in his left arm, his heart was still being monitored by the machine behind his bed, and a little plastic piece at his nose supplied oxygen. His bed was raised so he could watch TV, but his eyes were closed.

Bob came to the bedside and leaned over to him. "Doc?" he whispered.

A smile came to his lips, but his eyes remained closed. "Ah, son, look what they've done to me. One arm with an IV and the other with plaster of Paris. And the rest of me hooked up to a monitor. I'm beginning to think the good Lord lets us live too long."

"How do you feel?" Bob asked. He couldn't think of anything more appropriate.

"Is today Wednesday?" he asked ignoring Bob's question.

"Yes," he answered. Bob thought going on with the personal styles was out of the question. "Look, Doc—"

"Bob, listen to me. We have to finish what we've started."

"Let's put it on hold for right now," said Bob.

"No," said Dr. Crater. "Let's talk. I'll let you know when I'm too tired."

"But the nurse said I can only stay a short while."

"I'll be the judge of that," he snapped. Then with a smile, "I'm a *doctor*. Remember? Now, what's been happening?"

"Well, my secretary told me after the show

today, that the *Post-Dispatch* is aware of the format change. They have a reporter on it. Also, I talked with my accountant, Tom."

"Tell me more about Tom," said Crater.

Bob told him how Tom had asked him lots of questions, then analyzed various financial options depending on the outcome of Friday's meeting. Doctor Crater cut him off and said, "Get out your legal pad, but this time you write."

"Write what?"

"About Tom!" he said with some exasperation. "Don't you recognize another style when you see one?"

Bob hurriedly took his legal pad from his briefcase. He rolled the eating table away so Dr. Crater could see him comfortably and waited for Doc's instructions.

"Most effective traits," the doctor dictated. "Critical thinker. Detail oriented. Tactful. Precise/Accurate. Problem solver. Now, Bob, think of all the conversations you've had with Tom. When he discussed your income tax returns was he tactful asking how you spent your money? Did he press for details about the information you presented him? Now the *in*effective traits." Bob completed the chart.

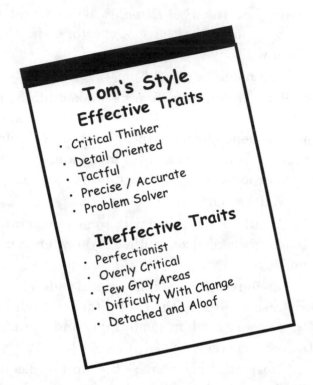

Tom's Style
Effective Traits

- Critical Thinker
- Detail Oriented
- Tactful
- Precise / Accurate
- Problem Solver

Ineffective Traits

- Perfectionist
- Overly Critical
- Few Gray Areas
- Difficulty With Change
- Detached and Aloof

"And what do we call this personal style?" asked Bob.

"Conscientiousness."

Bob reviewed Tom's traits, matching them with his most recent conversations. That was Tom all right: he displayed Conscientiousness; another word for Analyzer, he thought. He remembered Tom driving him up the wall one

74

year explaining the income tax reform. Yet, when it came to Bob's taxes, Tom let nothing slip through the cracks.

Dr. Crater lay there peacefully. The IV fluid was slowly sliding down its tube. The monitor behind the bed displayed an even rhythm. The TV was muted; just a flickering account of the world's news going by. As Bob sat there in the dimly lit room listening to the even breathing of the doctor, he wondered why it was so important for the doctor to share this knowledge.

"Bob," the doctor spoke, "we'll get to the fourth style tomorrow. But before you go, I want to tell you this." His voice was raspy. His throat dry. Bob poured fresh water into the glass, flexed a new straw, and brought it to his lips. The doctor took a sip, then another.

"Bob, the reason I gave you the effective and ineffective traits of each style is so you can identify when a person feels secure or insecure. If they show their worst traits, reassure them by complimenting one of their effective traits. That way you help them bring out their best qualities. Think of Tom. You asked his personal advice didn't you?"

"Yes, I did," said Bob. "But only because—"

"I'm not interested in *why* you asked. I'm interested in his answer. What did he say?"

"He said to follow my heart."

"He's right, but note how tactful that statement was. Look at Tom's chart again under effective traits."

Bob looked down on the chart. "It says tactful."

"So a compliment to Tom would acknowledge his tactfulness. He'll appreciate that because that's a valued trait of his. Whether a person displays effective or ineffective traits, you should *acknowledge* an effective trait. Remember, when people feel uncomfortable they are apt to exhibit their least effective traits. Work on that."

They were again silent for several minutes before Bob spoke.

"It seems so obvious when you explain it."

"Of course it is," he sighed, "it's as plain as the nose on your face. Don't you think insight into others will help you be a more effective communicator? Communication is your business, son. It's everybody's business. We communicate with people all our lives. Good leaders understand this.

"Bob, you are good at getting people to talk.

Now, as they talk, you'll be able to picture one of the charts I drew for you to quickly size them up. Then you *adapt* to how they communicate. And when you *acknowledge* their strong traits, they'll *really* talk to you. You can motivate them, inspire them, help bring out their strengths. Bob Hathaway, you have more talent than you know what to do with. It's that darned 'acceptance' thing with you that holds you back. Listen. If you focus on the other person, seek to find out what makes *that person* tick, you'll stop reacting and start acting like a leader. Whew! I'm spent," he said. "Get me some more water please."

Bob poured a fresh glass of water, popped in a new straw, and brought it to the doctor's lips. He noticed Dr. Crater's forehead had a veneer of perspiration. "Would you like me to get a cool cloth for your forehead?"

"Yes. That would feel nice."

Bob went to the bathroom and let the cold water run on the face cloth. He wrung it out, folded it in thirds, and brought it to the Doctor's bedside. Doc was asleep already, but Bob placed the cloth on his forehead anyway. A slight smile came across Doc's face, and then he drifted off again.

Bob said, "Doc, I always feel better for talking with you. I'll see you tomorrow." He didn't know if the doctor heard him, and he stayed a few moments longer before returning the face cloth to the rack in the bathroom.

Before leaving, Bob switched the TV to the old movie channel. If the doctor wanted to, he could watch something he saw at a time when life was more pleasant. And maybe for a little while it would take him out of the hospital, the IV, his broken wrist, and the hum of the heart monitor.

SEVENTEEN

Bob *WAS* BEGINNING to grow. He could feel it. He was consciously aware of his strengths and short-comings. He noticed he was more assertive without the annoying discomfort he'd felt in the past. Maybe he could stand in the eye of contro-versy. Maybe he would be the winner in Friday's showdown.

Appointments with clients and sales people kept him engaged till late in the afternoon on Thursday. It was 6:30 p.m. when he arrived at the hospital. Doc had been on his mind all day. He looked so very tired the last time Bob was there. While his mind was very alert and he could articulate his thoughts clearly, it just seemed his strength was leaving him. A comment Dr. Crater made lingered in Bob's mind: *"Sometimes I think the good Lord lets us live too long."*

He exited the elevator at the third floor and proceeded past the nurses' station to room 323. The door was open, the room was dark. But enough light came in from the hall that Bob could see the bed was empty. He thought for a moment the doctor might be in the bathroom, but as he scanned the night table he could see his water pitcher and get-well cards were gone.

"Excuse me," said a nurse.

Bob turned, "Where is Doctor Crater?"

"I'm sorry, but Doctor Crater passed away early this morning. Are you a member of his family?" she asked sympathetically.

"No, no," he muttered. "Just a friend." He stood there, shocked—not wanting to leave the room. "It was his heart?"

"Yes," she replied. "His son left information about arrangements. I can get that for you," she offered.

"Yes, thank you," replied Bob numbly. He followed her out of the room and down the hall to the nurses' station. She wrote out the name and phone number of the funeral home and handed the piece of paper to him.

"He was one of St. Louis' most respected

physicians," she said.

"Did you know him?" asked Bob.

"Not personally, only by reputation from some of the doctors who heard him lecture here at the hospital. He was an inspiration especially to the young interns," she said. "Weren't we lucky to have met him?"

"Yes. Yes, we were," said Bob looking up from the piece of paper.

"My name is Margaret. I'm one of the nurses who took care of him."

"My name is Hathaway."

"He spoke of you. Bob Hathaway? The one on the radio?"

He nodded.

"He thought very highly of you. He said—" and she paused.

"Tell me," said Bob.

"He said that you didn't know how *good* you are, or how great you could become."

Bob felt tears well up in his eyes. His throat constricted and he couldn't speak. He just nodded and tried to smile at Margaret, but his lips tightened trying to hold back the tears. He couldn't. They ran down his cheeks, and he began to sob. He reached out and patted the back of

Margaret's hand and quickly turned to the elevator. Alone in the elevator, great sobs started coming. He felt so terribly sad. Such a gentle man. As he walked through the lobby, he swallowed and clenched his teeth to contain the sorrow he felt. He just wanted to get outside—to let it out.

For nearly an hour he drove around the city—not wanting to go home—not wanting to go anywhere. But he soon was drawn to the Arch where he first met Dr. Crater.

The Arch is very majestic at night with the lights playing on the cold stainless steel. Standing there looking up at the tall monument and into the night sky, Bob felt very alone. He'd lost his mentor. Dr. Crater hadn't finished with what he'd set out for Bob. It was now up to him—to make his career decision by himself. *"You can't live your life for someone else,"* Doc had said.

He walked down the steps to the levee and stood in the midst of silent power: the Arch, the Cathedral, the River.

He sat on the steps where he'd first met Dr. Crater and looked out at the lights from East St. Louis. He played again in his mind the lessons the kind man had taught him, the wonderful wisdom that was making a difference in his life.

Two lovers walking by with their arms around each other's waist noticed the solitary figure lost in thought with a pleasant smile on his face. Bob had made his decision.

EIGHTEEN

IT WAS MIDNIGHT, and Bob was sitting in the club
chair in his living room sipping hot lemon and
honey tea. It was all coming together. All of Dr.
Crater's wisdom; clear and internalized. Bob had
grown, matured, and gained a confidence he had
never felt before. He always had confidence about
his work on-the-air, but now he had off-the-air
confidence as well. It was hard to explain, but it
was there. He could feel it.

He could click off the traits of Tom, of
Blaylock, and of himself effortlessly; effective and
*in*effective traits, strengths and weaknesses. He
hadn't experienced listening for these traits in
actual conversation, but he knew he would in
time, and it would help him be a more insightful
interviewer. Yes, he believed his future interviews

would be more than ferreting out facts; they would cut to a person's very core.

But what was the fourth style? Dr. Crater had spoken of four styles: Dominance, Influence, Conscientiousness, and—he couldn't think what the fourth one would be. Doc Crater didn't fit into any of the three styles he knew. While he did get to the bottom line, he didn't force that; he had patience. He was pleasant and social, but he wasn't overly so. He was a problem solver, but really gently prodded Bob to solve his own problem.

He finished his tea and set the cup and saucer on the table next to his chair. The hall clock chimed one o'clock, but he didn't want to go to bed even though he was weary; even though he had to face Blaylock at 7:30 a.m. His eyes closed and he dozed for a moment. He shook it off, trying to stay focused on the fourth personal style. He soon dozed again and fell asleep in the chair.

He awoke at three in the morning with a migraine headache. He cussed, rose heavily from the chair and went to the bathroom. He'd had these before; the sharp pain in his eye like a blunt ice pick. They always appeared during times of stress. He knew how to get rid of them. He pressed a hot face cloth against his face, smeared Vick's® around his eyes and nose, wrapped a towel around his head and sat upright, completely still, in complete darkness. With luck it would not reach the stage of vomiting; although that somehow opened the constricted blood vessels in his head and eased the pain more quickly. He felt he'd caught this one early enough and just sitting quietly in the dark would see him through. The clock in the hall chimed four. He'd made trips to the bathroom to re-apply the hot face cloth to his eye and forehead. The headache was slowly abating.

He turned his focus on Doc Crater's method of talking to him: how he asked questions, how he listened, how he made Bob think for himself, how he made Bob stretch. And Doc's appraisal of his potential: *"You don't know how good you are; you don't know how great you can be."*

Slowly he took the towel from his head. He heaved himself out of the chair, threw the towel into the air and shouted. "Yes, *he's* the fourth style: Doc Crater!"

He went to his desk and wrote out Dr. Crater's traits. He couldn't think of any least effective traits. There'd be time for that later. Right now, Bob was energized. His head was clear. He was ready for the Friday showdown

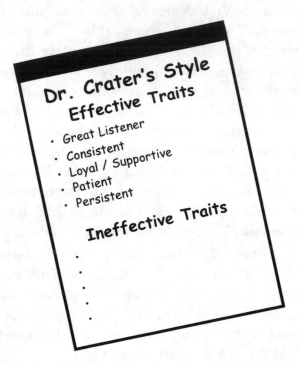

with Blaylock only two hours away. He had been dreading this meeting. But now—*now*—he could hardly wait for it to begin.

NINETEEN

At 7:25 A.M. he said good morning to Mr. Blaylock's secretary, Lorna. She told him the boss was on the phone and to have a seat. She offered him coffee, which he turned down. The double doors to the office were closed. Bob waited.

At 7:35 a.m. a voice came over the secretary's speaker phone. "Is Hathaway here?" She leaned to the speaker and said, "Yes, Mr. Blaylock."

Another five minutes passed before the doors opened and A.J., not even looking at Bob, said, "Come in, Hathaway."

Bob sat in the chair in front of Blaylock's desk. Blaylock stood with his back to him looking out the window at the Arch.

"Okay, let's have it," he said.

Bob took a deep breath and answered, "I won't

change the format."

Blaylock spun around, pushed his chair out of the way, braced his hands on his desk, leaned forward, and forced Bob to look up at him.

"What do you mean *you* won't change the format? That's a done deal. The new format starts Monday, and you're *it*," he snarled.

Bob stood up meeting him eye to eye. "You're not going to change me into something I'm not. My ratings are solid, and I'm attracting more people every day."

Blaylock cut him off. "So, you're Mr. Know-it-all. You think you know the pulse of this town? You haven't been here a full year yet. I'm telling you for your own good, the new format will make your star shine brighter than anyone's in this town. Sit *down*." Blaylock returned his chair to his desk and sat.

"We disagree, sir," said Bob, his heart pounding. He'd thrown down the gauntlet. He'd confronted.

Blaylock softened his tone; even smiled at Bob, and said, "Please sit down. Look Hathaway . . ."

"No, you look Mr. Blaylock," said Bob raising his voice while sitting reluctantly. "You hired me to do what I was doing successfully in another town. You *liked* that. You brought me here to repeat that success. Now you want to change it. If you want a controversial-shoot-from-the-lip talk host who alienates every one in town, if you want people tuning in to see how he'll skewer his guest or call-ins then you get a gun slinger."

Bob was full of himself. He'd never spoken like this to a boss. Never. *"You are your highest priority."* Dr. Crater's words were crashing through his mind.

"Don't be cute, Hathaway," said Blaylock. "If you don't have the guts to do the show, say so." He glared at Bob across the desk.

"You can't intimidate me, sir."

Blaylock turned in his chair and again faced the window. "Are you saying you would quit rather than go with the format change?"

Bob paused. Here was the moment of truth. This was the ultimate confrontation. The confrontation he'd thought about last night down on the levee. This was not a play where you could re-write the ending. Was he sure this is what he wanted? Had he gone too far? Was Blaylock about to fire him? Had he done his last show? Where would he go from here? There was a flicker of doubt. *"You don't know how good you are. You don't know how great you can be."* A wave of confidence restored him.

"Absolutely."

Blaylock spun back and faced Bob. "This is gross insubordination in my book, Hathaway. You leave here like this and you won't get a KXOR pedigree from me."

Bob leaned forward. "If I leave here, I leave with good ratings and a professional reputation."

"Let me make sure we're clear on this. You're telling me you won't continue to host the show under a new format."

"Correct."

"You're fired. Get out." He buzzed his secretary. "Lorna, bring me the dismissal forms."

Bob sat still. He wanted to ask what was next in the process. Was he to do his show today? But before he could ask, A.J. answered it for him.

"Leave. You're through. Get your stuff and get out of here. Your last show was yesterday."

Bob rose from the chair and headed for the door. As he reached it, he turned to Blaylock. He wanted to say something stunning, but he couldn't think of anything. So he simply scanned the room, nodding as he did, then left without closing the door.

He'd done a bold thing. He didn't know whether what he was feeling was euphoria or anxiety. He went upstairs to his office to tell Katie and asked her to box his things so he could pick them up Saturday morning when the staff wouldn't be around. She invited him to dinner with her family. He accepted.

In the stairwell, as he was leaving, Bob met the program director who had apparently not heard the news.

"Looking forward to Monday?" the program director asked.

"More than you know," Bob said. And with that, his career in St. Louis ended.

TWENTY

SUNDAY AFTERNOON, Bob attended Dr. Crater's funeral. He listened to Josh's warm and moving eulogy before the church full of people who had been touched by the great man: people from the hospital where Dr. Crater had looked in on patients, people from the University where he had lectured, and people who hadn't forgotten the medical wonders he'd provided for their infant sons and daughters.

Outside the church, after the service, Josh drew Bob aside and told him of the great respect his father had for him.

"Thank you," said Bob. "Your father was very special to me."

"Bob, I'd like you to meet my wife, Suzie, and our daughter, Alexandra." He led the way to where they were standing.

Bob expressed his sympathies to them and was delighted to hear Suzie say, "Why don't you come back home with us, Bob? After the things Doc told us about you, well, we consider you family."

Bob gladly accepted and followed them to their two storied, Dutch colonial home; white with black shutters. He admired the front porch with its white railings and an inviting settee you could swing on. Observing the orderliness of the flower beds that bordered the walkway to the porch steps, Bob took note of Josh's preference for things neat and well-planned.

Suzie, a tall and energetic woman, headed to the kitchen as Josh, Bob, and Alex sat in the family room.

Alex asked, "Mr. Hathaway? Will you go back to Miami to stay?"

Alex was a pretty girl, still a teenager, with an intense alertness about her.

"Well, Alex, I'll go back home now, but I have no idea where my next job will take me."

Yesterday's *Post-Dispatch* had featured Bob's "resignation" in the local section. Blaylock was quoted as saying, "As much as I wanted Bob

Hathaway to remain at KXOR, I could see the strain it was putting on him and his family. After much discussion, we mutually agreed to part company. To replace such a talented man, KXOR is conducting a nation wide search." The article spoke of the caliber of guests Hathaway attracted and how skilled an interviewer he was. It concluded with the note that Hathaway was unavailable for comment as he was en route to Miami. What the article didn't say was Bob *had* to agree with this "release" in a signed statement written by Blaylock under the veiled threat his severance might be delayed.

"Is it difficult to leave St. Louis?" Josh asked.

"Yes and no. It's been a strain not having the family here. You see, I didn't have a contract. Blaylock said a handshake was sufficient. So my wife and I decided to take a wait and see approach." He shook his head. "I wish they could have experienced St. Louis and all that it has to offer. What do you like best about St. Louis?" Bob asked diverting the subject from himself.

Josh said, "I'd really have to think about that. I enjoy the St. Louis Symphony, and, as you well know, we have our pick of first-run plays. I like the little esoteric presentations by the universities. Last year I saw a one-man show on the life of

Edgar Allen Poe. What do I like best about St. Louis? I guess I like St. Louis because there's always something first-rate to see."

"Alex?" Bob looked at the teenager whose posture was amazingly erect. "Tell me about your favorite thing to do."

"Horse back riding. A friend of mine owns a horse. His name is Royal, and I help her groom and exercise him." She laughed, "I even muck out the stable."

Suzie came in with a tray of coffee and some small cakes.

"Now, these are called divinity squares."

Bob took a bite. "Hmmm, they certainly live up to their name," he said. "These are delicious. Thank you."

Bob listened as Suzie entertained them with her adventures as a physical education teacher at the nearby high school. He could picture her at a ball field with a whistle around her neck yelling encouragement to her students. Bob could see that Suzie and Josh were a well balanced match: the methodical professor and the spontaneous motivator.

Suddenly, Alex excused herself, dashed out of the room, and headed for the stairs.

Suzie shook her head. "That girl is so impetuous—mind of her own—but I'm sure she'll be back." Smiling she asked, "So, you're off to Miami, Bob?"

"Yes, I'll be driving back in the morning. I'm not going to rush it. I need to wind down and think."

"I'll bet your family can hardly wait to see you," Suzie said.

Without warning, Alex came flying down the stairs. "I'm going to the movies," she said racing out the door.

"Who with dear?" called Suzie. There was no reply.

Josh heaved a sigh. There was a moment of discomfort before Suzie said, "Well, Bob, I guess you are all packed."

Bob could feel the tension in the room and thought it best to leave at the first convenient opportunity. Some ten minutes later, Bob thanked them both, gave Suzie a hug, and walked out to his car with Josh. He again expressed his sympathy to Josh as they said their good-byes.

When Bob returned to Miami, he applied to several major market radio stations including

WVB in Boston, whose management was so impressed with his air checks from KXOR, they offered him a two year contract. The opening was available immediately. So, in less than six weeks, he had a new job in a new city.

The whole family moved to Boston. His daughter fell in love with the swans gliding in the waters of the Public Garden. His son became a fan of another bird . . . the one called Larry, who glided over the parquet floor of Boston Gardens for the Celtics.

And now Bob would begin pleasing a new city, but with a different perspective. He knew his inner struggle with seeking acceptance would be uneven, but each day he focused on what he was, not what held him back. A new adventure had begun.

TWENTY-ONE

OVER THE NEXT YEAR, Bob felt a satisfaction with himself he had never known before. He no longer felt the need to be overly enthusiastic, just his natural optimism felt good. He no longer felt the need to exaggerate situations, just a normal account felt comfortable. He no longer sought out people's acceptance of him but instead felt confident with others and could enjoy their company. Sometimes he would get talky but was quick to recognize this ineffective trait and turn the conversation to the other person's interests. He focused more. He no longer feared confrontation. People liked to be around Bob because now he manifested something he had lacked before: substance. He was very happy in Boston.

Bob and Josh corresponded regularly, and in

Josh's most recent letter he indicated he would be coming to Boston to attend an engineering conference at Boston University. Bob was delighted and made dinner reservations for them at the hotel where Josh would be staying.

Bob drove to Logan Airport to meet him. He stood at the gate and watched the TWA flight from St. Louis taxi to the terminal. He was looking forward to seeing his mentor's son once again. Bob watched the ramp, and when Josh entered the terminal Bob raised his arm to signal him.

Now, they sat across the table from each other talking about their careers when Josh abruptly changed the subject.

"Bob, I need to know more about the personal styles. You know, what my Dad shared with you."

"Certainly," Bob said passing his napkin across his lips. "But first tell me what you know about them."

Josh hesitated.

"Did your Dad discuss them with you?"

"Well," said Josh, "he did. But," and he lowered his head, "I'm embarrassed to say I didn't pay a whole lot of attention. You know how you're apt to shrug off stuff your parents tell you."

Bob nodded and smiled.

"I guess now I'm ready to listen, and I'd like to hear how *you* explain them."

"Well, let me tell you about my introduction to the four styles. First there was Blaylock's style. Your Dad told me his was Dominance. I thought he was a dictator. At the time I saw only his pit bull side. He was blunt, argumentative, never really listened to what anybody else had to say. So to me, he was a hostile, dictatorial kind of guy. I never saw him with his peers, never saw the traits that made him so successful. If I had, I would have seen his presidential side: a results oriented, lover of challenges, direct and self-assured person. Looking back, I must admit when he first hired me, he was indeed presidential; couldn't have been nicer. So I learned from your father that each style has effective and ineffective traits. In Blaylock's case presidential and dictatorial; both under the style of Dominance.

"Tom was my accountant who helped me at that time. His style was Conscientiousness. He was as detail-oriented as they come. I've met hundreds of Toms and so have you."

Josh smiled. "Every time I look in the mirror."

Bob blinked. "Then you agree that while we

admire their absolute devotion to detail, their tactfulness, their critical thinking, and their problem solving ability, they can drive us up the wall by *over analyzing* a subject, or being aloof, or procrastinating over making a decision. They can be a cautious analyzer, or a tactful diplomat. Two sides of Tom and both under the style of Conscientiousness. Are you getting the picture?"

Josh nodded. "Got it. One style, two sets of traits. Why do we have two sets of traits?"

"I'll come to that in just a minute."

Bob couldn't put his finger on the reason for it, but he heard an unnatural urgency in Josh's tone.

"Let me tell you about the other two styles. Mine was Influence. Now, I knew I had strong communication skills, persuasive powers, and success in entertaining people. But I was not aware of being gabby, *overly* enthusiastic, and avoiding confrontation for the sake of being accepted. I knew about the acceptance drive in me, but I didn't know any other way to live. When I was 'strong' I was a great communicator. When I was 'weak,' I was a pleaser. Two sides of me, too. Both under the Influence style."

"And the fourth style?" Josh interrupted.

"Ah, that was your Dad. I saw only one side of Doc: the great listener, consistent, patient, persistent, and a supportive friend. His was Steadiness. Only later, in other people, did I discover the least effective traits of the Steadiness style: highly sensitive, passive, indecisive, overly tolerant, and uncomfortable with change. Maybe your Dad was never troubled with these ineffective traits. Then again, maybe he was as a young man. But the point is: the Steadiness style has two sides, too."

"How can you be two people in one?" Josh asked.

"You've heard the expressions: 'She's beside herself.' 'He's not himself today.' That's when the ineffective traits dominate our behavior, but when the world is going our way we confidently display our most effective attributes. We say: 'She's on her best behavior.' 'He's putting his best foot forward.' Both sets of expressions reflect the duality of our personal style.

"Understand the styles, Josh, and you understand others. But the biggest revelation is understanding who *you* really are." Bob watched Josh fidget with his silverware then continued, "So, Josh, why the sudden interest in the styles?"

There was something Josh wasn't telling him. If that was the case, it was Josh who had to bring it out. The waiter came with some after-dinner coffee.

"Is that decaf?" asked Bob.

The waiter assured him it was.

"Because if it's not, I'll be up half the night." He turned to Josh whose look of intensity had dissolved into the face of a beaten man. "Bob," Josh sighed. "The main reason I came to Boston was not the engineering conference. I have a big problem at home, and I don't know what to do or where to turn. I don't have Dad to talk with anymore."

Bob leaned forward but remained quiet; waiting. Josh looked away, "Bob, it's Alexandra, my seventeen year old daughter. She's . . . run away."

TWENTY-TWO

B<small>OB</small> <small>ASKED.</small> "Do you know where she is?"

"Yes. She's staying with another family. A family we've never heard mentioned before."

"How did this happen?"

"She's been secretive recently. Dashing in and out of the house. Going to see this friend and that. School friends she says. Never has them to the house, so we don't know them."

"And she just ran away? Just like that out of a clear blue sky?"

"This past year, Bob, we've had a hard time communicating with her. The night before she left, we had a talk at the supper table. We wanted to know about her friends; wanted to know why she was so abrupt with us. We accomplished nothing. It turned out to be an angry talk. The next day, we called the school's guidance counselor and asked if she could come to the house after school. When Alex came home, we told her the counselor would be coming. Alex went to her room. When the counselor arrived, I went to ask Alex to join us. Her bedroom door was locked, but I heard rattling going on at her window. When I came back to the living room to tell Suzie, I saw Alex running down the street. I ran outside and called to her. A car picked her up at the end of the street, and she was gone."

"How did you find out where she was staying?" asked Bob.

"She called that evening. She told us she'd be all right, not to worry, not coming home, has to work some things out . . . and don't try to find her."

"But how *did* you find her?" Bob persisted.

"I hired a private detective, and he found the address. Then we went to the police. They told us who she was living with."

"Did they offer to get her back?"

"Well, here's the dicey situation. Alex is very head strong. What good would forcibly bringing her back do? She'd be gone, who knows where, the first time we turned our back. This way, she's safe, going to school, and, as she says, 'working things out.'

"The family where she's staying called, introduced themselves, and assured us she'll be all right. They also, politely, warned us not to try to bring her home. Can you imagine that? This is crazy!"

"So what are you doing about it?"

"We're doing what the police suggested. We're waiting it out."

"The police told you to wait it out?" Bob asked incredulously.

"They told us with all the teenage problems they deal with, this one is minor."

Bob shook his head.

After a pause Josh asked, "Got any answers?"

Bob took a deep breath. "Do you have *any* contact with her at all?"

"She calls on weekends."

Josh sat back in his chair, his hands in his lap.

Gently Bob asked, "Why do *you* think she ran away?"

"I wish I knew," Josh shrugged. "Ever since she became a teenager we've had a lack of communication; no connection whatsoever. She's been impatient with me. Nothing I say seems to come out right. But I thought this was just a normal part of growing up."

Bob watched Josh put cream and sugar into his coffee meticulously. It was best, he thought, to remain silent and let Josh continue when he was ready.

Josh took a sip from his cup, returned it to the saucer carefully, then sat back in his chair. He didn't look directly at Bob, but stared absently at his coffee cup.

"I've never seen her so angry as she was two months ago," said Josh. "Maybe it's because I'm a school teacher, and an engineer to boot, but when she was little and asked me a question, I always responded with a one, two, three answer. I thought that was the logical way to respond and the easiest for her to understand.

"Anyway, Suzie and I started sending for college catalogues. Alex appeared disinterested, so Suzie and I talked it up a lot. One night Alex asked me why it was so important for her to go to

110

college. I said, 'Alex the reasons are simple: Number one . . .' That's as far as I got. She says, 'Oh, you always have a one, two, three answer for everything.' Bob, she screamed it at me and stomped out of the room."

"Josh, she would have been upset no matter how you approached it." Bob put both hands on the table and leaned closer. "I think it goes deeper. I think she's more frustrated with the *way* in which you talk with her. Here's the communication pattern you've established with Alex: 'What's your question, here's your answer, end of conversation.'

"Josh, when she came to you over the years with questions, I don't think she wanted an answer so much as she wanted a discussion with you so she could express herself. She wanted you to listen to her. Your way offered no discussion possibilities. I know you didn't mean it to come out that way, but it did. Father knows best when he gives his tongue a rest and just listens."

Josh shook his head. "And I'm a college professor."

"Josh, they don't give out manuals on *Bringing up Alex.*"

They paused, Bob again letting Josh set the pace of the conversation. Sometimes it was very difficult for Bob to remain silent, but he learned this discipline from Doc Crater. One of his ineffective traits was: he talked too much. Well, he was neutralizing that trait right now, though the silence was unbearable. He leaned back in his chair.

"Bob," said Josh hesitantly, "can you help me?"

"What's your biggest fear?"

Josh thought for a moment. "Fear of losing her because I don't understand her."

"Then, let's focus on that."

"Bob, that's why I asked you about the styles." Josh's voice rose. "I thought if I knew her style, I could understand her; could make a connection with her." His frustration showed as he said somewhat bitterly, "What good are these styles if I can't *apply* them?"

Oh, good question. It stopped Bob's thought process momentarily. But then he focused on the immediate concern: how to establish a dialogue between Josh and Alex.

"Well, first things first," said Bob. "Let's determine her style."

"How do I do that?"

"Get her talking."

"Bob, I'm not much of a conversationalist. How do I get her talking?"

"Interview her."

"What do you mean, interview her?"

"Let me give you some tips to get Alex talking and keep her talking. I do this for a living, you know."

"Should I take notes?"

Bob grinned. "It wouldn't hurt."

Josh signaled the waiter and asked if he could have a pad to write on.

TWENTY-THREE

"**J**OSH, ONE OF THE THINGS I do best is get people talking. Some of the salespeople at the radio station have asked me how I do that. I've told them, and they use my techniques to get their prospects talking so they can figure out their needs.

"Alex wants you to listen to her, but you can't listen unless she talks. It's your responsibility to learn how to get her talking. The next time you speak with Alex, begin your conversation with, 'Tell me about . . . .'"

Josh wrote down the words 'Tell me about.'

"Now, let me tell you why these three words are magic. If Alexandra returned from a movie and you asked, 'How was the movie?' She might answer, 'Fine.' A one word answer won't do, so you ask, 'What did you think of the movie?' She responds, 'I thought it was fine.' So far two questions and, in essence, two one word answers. You try again. 'How did you feel about the movie last night?' She says, 'I felt it was fine and why are you grilling me with all these questions?' But, Josh, if you phrased the question this way: *Tell me about* the movie you saw last night,' you won't get a one word answer; you'll get a paragraph and maybe more."

"That's good," said Josh.

"Here's step two: Signposts."

Josh drew a line across the page under 'Tell me about,' then wrote Signposts.

"Josh, put down the pen. Just listen to me for a moment. While Alex is answering your first 'tell me about . . .' question, listen for signposts. These are topic words that help you concentrate on what she's saying so you can ask another question to keep her talking. It's simple to pick out *signposts*. Let me give you an example with a nursery rhyme.

> *"Jack and Jill went up the hill*
> *To fetch a pail of water.*
> *Jack fell down and broke his crown,*
> *And Jill came tumbling after.*

"Let's say you and Jack are at a meeting that night. You notice the bandage around his skull and say, 'Jack, tell me about your accident.' You lean forward and look expectantly. Jack begins.

"Well, I was going up the hill, you know how I always do, to get a pail of water. Jill was with me. When we reached the top of the hill, I primed the pump and filled up my bucket. Just as I turned to start down the hill, Jill pointed up to the sky and said, 'Jack, look at the airplane.' I looked up and saw a skywriter spelling out the word Pepsi in the sky. I lost my balance and started tumbling down the hill elbows over tea kettles. I whacked my head on a rock and had to go to Doc Winslow's for four stitches. Jill? She came tumbling after. She's at the chiropractor's now."

"Josh. How many *signposts* are in Jack's answer? Count them. Jack, Jill, Hill, Water, Bucket, Pump, Airplane, Sky, Skywriter, Pepsi, Rock, Accident, Doctor, Chiropractor."

"That's fourteen said Josh.

"Yes. Fourteen *signposts* for you to easily ask another *'Tell me about . . .'* question."

Josh thought for a moment, then asked, "So you choose the signpost you want to talk about?"

"Exactly. You are the guide of the conversation."

They both took a respite to reflect on the information. Then Bob said, "You're an engineer, Josh. How would you design a picture of a conversation?"

"A picture?"

"Yes, draw me a picture of a conversation."

Josh hesitated. Then he picked up his pen and placed it over the pad. Nothing.

"Can't think of anything," he said, slightly embarrassed.

Bob leaned forward and with his hands framed a picture. "Josh, draw a frame, then make a target with a bull's-eye."

Josh made a square, then a circle with a bull's-eye in the center.

"The outer circle represents business information, the inner circle represents personal information. The business information is what Alex is doing: the school she goes to, the classes she takes, her schedule, her material needs and so forth. The personal information reflects her values, her dreams, her thoughts, her innermost self. Now what can you determine from gathering this information?"

"Her personal style," answered Josh breaking into a smile.

"Bull's-eye!" said Bob.

It was getting late. Josh had risen early to make the flight from St. Louis, and it was now 11:30 p.m. Bob asked if Josh wanted to pick this up later.

"Absolutely not!" he replied. "This is golden. If it's all right with you, let's keep going."

They ordered more decaf and some warm apple pie with cheddar cheese on the side.

"What's the third step?" asked Josh.

"Brief inserts," said Bob. "When Alexandra is telling you something, don't interrupt her train of thought."

"And I do that by . . .?"

"By using words like: 'oh,' 'wow,' 'I see.' I call these brief inserts. A perfect example of someone who does not interrupt is Larry King. He asks a question and listens to his guest's answer. He doesn't, as some do, try to insert *his* beliefs or a story about *him* to support the guest's point. He simply nods or uses a *brief insert*. This does three things: it shows the guest he's paying attention, it lets Larry hear more signposts for a wider range of questions and, thirdly, it gets the guest talking and revealing more about themselves. To keep Alexandra talking, use *brief inserts*."

"Where did you learn all this stuff?" asked Josh taking a sip of coffee.

"When I was at KXOR, one of my guests was Leo Buscaglia. After our interview he said, 'You really listen!' I was flattered by that and, later, analyzed the steps I was using to get people talking. That's how I came up with this interview process.

"So far," Bob continued, "we've covered three steps: *Tell me about*, to start the conversation; s*ignposts* to grab topic words to guide the conversation and keep it going; and *brief inserts* to not interrupt the flow of information.

"The fourth step is the *pause*. This is the greatest interview tip I can give you. After Alex has finished her response, *pause*. There'll be a slight discomfort during the silence, but this is what will happen. Alex will continue talking, revealing personal information; the kind of information you would never know to ask about. She will let her *personal* feelings come out. Bull's-eye. The *Pause* is your greatest ally in determining her style and for discovering what's on her mind."

Bob cut into a piece of pie before he continued.

"I remember reading a *New York Times* book

review on Edward R. Murrow. The biographer documented how the revered CBS journalist conducted his interviews. He asked a question, got an answer, and then just remained silent. Guess what? The person he was interviewing talked more—said things that Murrow would have never known to ask—and *that* is what they used on the air. Why? Because that was the essence of the person's thoughts and feelings."

"I've never thought of that," said Josh.

"Here's the final element in any conversation. The summary. Always *summarize* at the conclusion of your conversation. This applies to Alex, your students, or anyone you are talking with. Summarize what you've accomplished and what the next step will be.

"And you know what happens when you truly listen to someone, Josh? You unconsciously use your most effective traits—your best 'self.'"

Bob knew he had given Josh a lot to digest.

"Oh my, it's one o'clock," said Josh rising, his hands on his waist as he arched his back. "Do you realize we've been sitting here talking for seven hours. Seven hours! Can you believe that?"

As they walked out of the restaurant, Bob asked, "Josh, have you seen the latest issue of

Fortune magazine?"

"No, why?"

"Pick it up before you go home. It has a very interesting cover story. The editors surveyed several of the *Fortune* 500 CEOs and asked them what it will take to excel, in fact survive, in the years ahead. The consensus was: *The leader of today must learn to listen to understand what makes people tick.*"

They both stopped, looked at each other and in unison said, "Bull's-eye!"

TWENTY-FOUR

THREE MONTHS PASSED, and Bob often thought about Josh's frustrated remark, 'What good are the styles if you can't apply them.'

Bob knew the knowledge of styles was helpful to understand another person. "But how do I let that person *know* I understand him?" he muttered as he paced in his study. "That is what's missing. If I could create a connection process, then I could help Josh connect with Alex; salespeople connect with clients; managers connect with associates."

The phone interrupted him. It was Josh.

"Alex has come home," he shouted.

"Great news! Tell me about it," said Bob as he sat in his club chair.

"Well, as soon as I arrived home from our meeting, I tried your suggestions during her weekend calls. I'd ask her to tell me about something at school. Then I'd listen, pick up a signpost and ask her about that. When she'd finish, I'd pause, and, you were right, she kept on talking."

"How long did it take before you could touch on her personal thoughts and feelings?"

"I'm still afraid to broach that. I'm just happy she's home!"

"Did she just pop in?"

"Well, last month she started visiting us on the weekends. She laid out the ground rule that we were not to persuade her to stay."

"How did you feel about that?"

"Uncomfortable—like walking on eggs. Conversation was forced."

"What made her decide to come back to stay?"

"I don't know."

"Do you still feel uncomfortable?"

"Yes. She flat out said if things don't go well, she'll move out again. It's still a strain. No connection yet."

"How is Suzie handling it?"

"Pretty well for the most part, but they get into it. Like when Suzie says, 'eat your veggies,' Alex storms out of the kitchen."

Bob paused waiting for Josh to resume.

"Maybe you think I should be firmer. Maybe you think she needs a good shaking, but that would only drive her away again. You want to know something Bob?"

"What?"

"I was looking at the styles you talked about when we met. I think there's a little Blaylock in her," he said wryly.

"Dominance?"

"I think so. She's blunt, and she's dictating some rules. But I also see something I like very much. She's very self-assured."

"Interesting," said Bob. "But still no revealing personal information?"

"I'm not making much headway on that."

"What are you doing?"

"I tell her how proud I am of her, but I still can't crack that wall."

Bob leaped from his chair. "What do you say exactly?"

"What words do I use?"

"Yes."

"I say, 'Alex, I'm proud of what you're accomplishing at school.'"

"Telling her you are proud of her only reinforces she's still a child in your mind. Lift her to your level. That's what she wants, Josh. She wants you to see her as an equal and independent adult. She wants to express her individuality."

"What am I suppose to say?"

Bob thought for a moment. "Get out your notes on the styles." Bob was speaking rapidly as ideas were taking shape in his mind. "Look at the effective traits of the Dominance style. When you see her manifesting any of those traits, verbally acknowledge that trait. It's the finest compliment you can give her."

"Yes," said Josh slowly. "Acknowledge her individuality. Why that's the finest compliment you can give *anyone*."

Bob quickly said goodbye, grabbed a legal pad and began to write. The major breakthrough was here at last: combining the styles with a connection process. With joy he wrote at the top of the page: "How to connect with anyone . . . including yourself!"

TWENTY-FIVE

Spring is a time of rebirth. While seasons come and go with perfect predictability, people's lives are perfectly unpredictable. If Doc Crater were looking down, he would note with satisfaction that Bob was about to make an unpredictable, self-realizing decision—an astonishing rebirth.

After accepting an invitation from some independent insurance agents to speak at their monthly meeting, Bob decided to share his interviewing techniques to help them get prospects talking to better determine their insurance needs.

Not only did he receive complimentary letters afterwards but he received more requests for speaking engagements. These led to expanding his talk to a half-day seminar. He called them

Saturday Seminars for he found combining the interview process with personal styles was a natural and vital correlation. Several companies in Massachusetts hired him, and by mid-summer he was addressing audiences in Maine and New Hampshire. The word was out: Bob Hathaway was a good presenter with sound material. And more, Bob Hathaway found a new calling.

Meanwhile, at the New England Broadcasters Association Banquet in July, Bob took great pride in being honored as best interviewer in Boston and, later that month, in a national poll, one of the top interviewers in America. Yet as much as he loved his job, a voice inside him kept saying, "It's time to move on."

In late August he received a letter from Josh. Alex had graduated from high school and had decided not to go to college; opting instead to enter the work force. She wanted a career in real estate and had joined a local firm as a broker trainee. Since Suzie and Josh were college graduates, they were naturally disappointed with her decision. "It's her decision, but I hope she'll change her mind," he wrote.

He also mentioned the improved relationship with his daughter. He appreciated all Bob's help; particularly, the connection blueprint. "That really brought us together," he concluded.

Bob thought back to when Josh had said, "What good are the styles if you can't apply them." Bob was fleshing out the answer to that question as he prepared his new *all-day* seminar. He could hardly wait to get home each day to work on it.

Driving home one day in September, taking in the rich vista of New England's autumn spectacle, he could feel a passion within him—a powerful drive to tell the world what Dr. Crater had taught him about the styles. He thought, if people knew "who they were," they could knock down their roadblocks. Helping Josh, he discovered the linkage between what Dr. Crater had taught him about the styles and how to apply that knowledge. What a boon that would be for new graduates, husbands and wives, salespeople, managers, in fact, everyone who dealt with people. And the encouragement he received from his Saturday Seminars justified his motivation in this direction.

It was the first time in his life he had thought of being in business for himself. Why follow someone else's destiny when you can create your own, he thought. The prospect excited him.

It was no longer vital that he *be* liked. Rather, it was important to him to *do* what he liked. He liked radio, but this all-consuming motivating force to help people understand themselves, understand others, and know how to connect with others to build stronger business and personal relationships was something he could not stop.

His contract renewal with WVB was only six months away. The thought of staying in radio paled against what he was contemplating. Was this what Dr. Crater meant when he said, "You don't know how great you can be." It was an enormous step he was considering. Perhaps the biggest decision of his life. He was fifty years old! Should he take the risk?

He recalled a *Wall Street Journal* survey of people over sixty-five. The survey asked: If you had it to do all over again, what would you do differently? The number one response was they would have taken more risks in their careers.

Bob had taken risks before, but this was a big one. He asked himself, what's my biggest fear? "The fear of failure," he said aloud.

He remembered a question Dr. Robert Schuller had asked in one of his sermons, "What great thing would you attempt if you knew you could not fail?"

When he arrived home, Bob talked with his wife. He was very fortunate to have a mate who believed in him more than he believed in himself. He knew she had vision; she could see what was ahead for him when he could not. And now, when he expressed his thoughts of not renewing his radio contract and focusing full time on a seminar business, she urged him to go in business for himself. "Do it, Bob," she had said.

It was a bitter cold January morning when Bob pulled into the radio station parking lot. The reality of what he was about to do suddenly came over him. He thought, in fifteen minutes I'll be telling the station's manager, John Pratt, I'm leaving. Can I really be chucking a successful twenty-five year career to start at the bottom of something new? He turned the ignition off, took out the key, and sat there gathering his thoughts for a moment.

"That's it," he muttered getting out of the car. "I've made my decision. Like Doc said, I'm my highest priority."

The winter wind made his eyes water. He

scrunched his neck into his overcoat and hurried into the radio station.

John Pratt welcomed him into his office. On the cream colored walls were pictures of early Boston. Behind his oak desk was a picture looking down the street to the old North Church. A statue of Paul Revere stood on his credenza, and across the room, by the window, was a grouping of two chairs and a sofa in colonial yellow fabric separated by an antique coffee table.

"Have a seat, Bob," he said motioning to the sofa. "Would you like some coffee?"

"Yes, please."

John went over to the silver coffee thermos on the credenza.

"How do you like it?"

"Cream and one sugar," Bob replied.

Handing Bob his coffee, he took a seat in the chair across from him.

"What's on your mind?" he asked.

"I'm thinking of leaving the radio business." He waited for John to speak.

"Is it money we're talking about here, Bob?"

"No, this isn't a ploy for an increase, John. I've found a new challenge in the seminar business. I have to try it. If I stay on, I fear I'll be doing both of us a disservice." He paused for a sip of coffee.

John went to his desk for a legal pad and brought it back to his chair. He wrote a headline, drew a line down the center of the page, and started writing under each column. Bob watched, but said nothing. He respected John Pratt, and he knew him to be a good listener, a patient man, but a persistent administrator.

When John finished, he passed the pad to Bob. The headline read, "Bob Hathaway's Future." One column was titled WVB, the other, SEMINARS. The WVB column had many items citing his success, his stature in the community, his salary, his benefits, his twenty-five year investment. The other column was empty save for a little question mark.

John waited patiently for Bob to respond.

Bob had finished reading, but held his gaze on the list and thought again of the decision at hand. He felt a tension similar to that which he felt in Blaylock's office when he realized the conversation had gone beyond the point of no return. He knew whatever he said next would take him beyond that point again.

Doubts coursed through his mind. It would be so easy to say, 'I'll stay.' But how will I feel tomorrow morning if I decide to stay? Will I regret not taking a chance on myself? On the other hand, will I miss rubbing elbows with the celebrities I interview? Can I handle the absence of a regular pay check? How will I feel about *that* when I wake up tomorrow?

John spoke. "Would you like to take more time to make your decision?"

As though directed by an inner voice, he pushed himself up from the sofa and walked over to the statue of Paul Revere on the credenza. Touching the statue of the legendary silversmith he said, "John, do you recall the name of anyone who interviewed Paul Revere?"

His blank look said it all.

Bob extended his hand. "John, I've made my decision."

TWENTY-SIX

THE BIG DELTA JET carrying Bob Hathaway
landed smoothly on the runway in Orlando. Bob
watched the passengers, mostly vacationers and
their children, talk excitedly about Disney World
as the plane rolled up to the gate. Bob was
excited, too. He was here to present the first
major seminar of his new career.

Thirty days after he left WVB, he received a
letter from a large brokerage firm asking if he
were available to conduct his seminar before
eight hundred and fifty of their brokers. Eight
hundred and fifty! He couldn't believe his good
fortune. Yes, he was available.

He created workbooks. He fine tuned and
rehearsed each module of the seminar. If I fail, he
told himself, it won't be for lack of preparation.

The week before he left, he called Josh.

"Congratulations," he said when Bob told him the good news. "When is it?"

"Next Saturday in Orlando."

"Can I come?"

"Of course you can."

"I'll fly in Saturday morning. What hotel, Bob?"

"I'm sorry. It's the Clarion Plaza."

Josh *had* to hear Bob's seminar. A seminar that his father had unknowingly set into motion. A seminar that he himself had contributed to because of a family problem.

The first thing Bob did, when he checked in, was ask if his workbooks had arrived. "Yes, they have, Mr. Hathaway," said the desk clerk. Bob breathed a sigh of relief, signed the register, and went up to his room. After unpacking, he called room service for supper, went over his notes, and then to bed. Tomorrow he would show the brokers how to connect with anyone . . . including themselves.

TWENTY-SEVEN

THE MORNING SESSION was complete, and Bob was pleased to hear them chatting about their styles: Dominance, Influence, Steadiness, and Conscientiousness as all eight hundred and fifty stock brokers filed out of the ballroom and headed for lunch.

Several of the brokers stayed to ask questions. "How can I stop being who I am?" asked one.

Bob answered, "You don't stop being who you are. Rather, it's understanding and focusing on your effective traits and being aware of and learning to overcome those traits that hold you back. That's how you begin to fulfill your potential."

He was patient with questioners, but finally suggested they go to lunch, or they would be late for the afternoon session. He looked around the emptying room for Josh. Not seeing him, he turned back to the stage area and started putting his notes back in his briefcase.

"Are you the young man starting a new career?"

Bob spun around. And there, looking up to the stage and beaming at him was Josh.

"Josh, you son of a gun, it's good to see you." Bob jumped off the stage and put his arm around Josh's shoulder and shook his hand.

Bob couldn't wait to tell him. "I wish you could have seen the brokers respond to the personal styles. It was a magical revelation," he said with excitement.

As they walked to the restaurant Josh said, "Look at you in your blue suit and French cuffs. Very corporate. I can see that being in business for yourself agrees with you."

Bob smiled. "It shows, doesn't it? You know, Blaylock was the greatest thing that happened to me. Everyone should have a Blaylock. Someone who forces you to take stock and make a personal decision. But I couldn't have done it without the support and knowledge of your father. Everyone should have a Crater, too. Two Craters, in fact. If it weren't for your coming to me with Alex's mis-adventure, I don't think I would have discovered the *connection* part. That's the most important aspect of any relationship: business or personal."

They were seated in the hotel restaurant now, and Josh asked, "So, why did the stock brokers ask you to hold a seminar for them?"

"They have difficulty relating to their clients. It's amazing. These brokers—whose very existence is predicated on understanding people—rarely have this training. They get a job in a brokerage house, spend an inordinate amount of time studying the equities market and hardly ever study people! Look, I can buy shares of General Electric from a full service broker, a discount broker, buy them direct from GE, and even buy shares on-line on my computer. The product isn't what's going to bring me into the broker's office, it's the broker! The individual is the determining factor."

He shook his head and continued.

"I once asked the head of a law firm what their greatest need was. You know what he said?" Bob paused. "He said, 'Our attorneys know every-thing about law and nothing about dealing with people. They don't know how to relate to the client.' Does that tell you something? This lack is rampant across industry. You'd think the school system would teach people skills."

"If they did, you'd be out of business."

Bob laughed. "I guess you're right."

"I'm looking forward to seeing how you put all this together. What do you do?"

"I show them how to apply the styles."

"By . . ."

"Well, the first step is to teach them how to get people talking."

"The interview process," Josh said as he thought of how it helped him become a better father. "That's critical."

"Absolutely! When salespeople *only* recite a presentation, they learn absolutely nothing about the prospect or client because they've been doing all the talking. That's a big flaw. *Big* flaw! Out in the parking lot, they wonder why they didn't get the sale. Their sales manager often tells them they didn't close right. So they focus on closing. They should be focusing on gathering business and personal information!

"Same thing applies if you're a manager. To motivate employees, find out what makes them tick and direct them to a project that best compliments the effective traits of their personal style.

"It's an advantage to know a person's style. Helps you get on his or her wave length. And the way to do that is to guide the conversation back and forth from business to personal information just like the target we drew in Boston. Do you remember the picture of a conversation?"

"Indelibly," said Josh forcefully. "You must get *all* the information."

Bob continued. "The second step is to *determine* their style by what they've said. The third step is to *adapt* to their individual traits."

"Fill me in on that," said Josh. "This is like an anatomy of a conversation."

"Sure. Respond to the person in his or her style. That's adapting. Remember Blaylock's style? He was a direct, no-nonsense kind of guy. A bottom-liner, right?"

"Right."

"That's precisely how to respond to him. You don't go into great detail, you don't tell him stories. Blaylock just wanted the facts, so you adapt to his style."

Josh chuckled.

"What's so funny?" smiled Bob.

"That's exactly what I did with my daughter. She liked the short, get-to-the-point 'tell me about' questions of the Dominance style. It was all right for *her* to talk as long as she wanted, but not me. To deal with her style, I had to keep my questions and comments short and simple."

"And it worked, didn't it?"

"Definitely. She liked me to listen to her."

"By the way, how is Alex doing?"

"She has a new career," said Josh proudly.

"Oh?"

"Tell you about it tonight. By the way, I'm treating you to supper."

They left the restaurant and headed back to the ballroom.

"We didn't get to the fourth step," said Josh.

"That's what the afternoon session is about."

"How do you think the seminar is going?"

They ducked into an alcove. "Josh, I'm uneasy—like I used to feel before a final exam. My future is dependent on the success of the breakthrough connection process. This client is huge. If I succeed today, this can take me to the *Fortune* 500 companies. If I fail, I'm out of business."

"Bob, what's your fear?"

"Josh," he said with some exasperation, "this is not the time to talk about that." He started down the hall, then stopped and turned back. "I *will* tell you. I fear if I fail, I will end up being a disc jockey out in the boondocks playing big band music."

"Bob, turn around."

"Why?"

"Just turn around," said Josh putting his hands on Bob's back.

"What are you doing?"

"I'm removing the baggage from your back," said Josh pretending to struggle with a heavy load. "I just removed the entire big band era."

Bob turned and faced Josh laughing.

"Now, go in there and knock their socks off," said Josh. "I'll find a seat in the back of the room."

Bob entered the ballroom. Josh, however, did not go in. Instead he headed down the hallway toward the hotel lobby. He appeared to be looking for someone.

TWENTY-EIGHT

THE BUZZ IN THE ROOM abated and the brokers applauded as Bob took the stage that featured a rear screen projector, a small table, and a tall stool.

"This afternoon," he began, "I want to show you how to apply your knowledge of personal styles to make each business meeting a success. We'll define success as *connecting* with the prospect or client."

The word appeared on the screen behind him.

Connecting

"Let me give you an example of *connecting* with someone. Let's say you tell me you want to buy a red Mustang convertible, and you're going

145

to visit three Ford Dealers. You return and say:

"They're all alike; same layout, same number of cars, even the same price."

I ask which of the three you're going to buy your car from.

You say, "The second one, because the salesman and I *hit it off*."

"But what about the others? Surely they were professional salespeople."

"True," you say, "but the first salesman kept asking me what it would take to put me in a car *today*. The third kept telling me how great I'd look in the car. It was the second salesperson, however, that *connected*. I felt as though he knew me."

"Now, let's analyze what the second salesman did to *connect*. He *interviewed* you (got you talking about business and personal information). He *determined* your style. Then he *adapted* to your personal style and, finally, *acknowledged* a trait from your style. You felt the *connection*. He made the sale!

"*Acknowledging* the style trait of the person you're talking with is the final step.

"If I compliment you on your tie or jewelry, I've said something positive about your *taste*. But if I compliment you on *you*, I've offered the *supreme* compliment. In other words, I've recognized a quality beyond your taste, or manners, or etiquette, or your hairdo, or your shiny new car. I've recognized the very essence of you. Not only have I recognized it, but I've verbally *acknowledged* it. I've acknowledged you as being a get-the-job-done-now kind of person, or being great with people, or being as steady as a rock, or being a stickler for details. This is powerful stuff!

Connecting
The 4 Step process

- **Interview** to get people talking

- **Determine** personal style

- **Adapt** to the personal style

- **Acknowledge** the style trait

"Acknowledging a personal style trait is *the connector*. It says to that person that you've listened to them and have discovered their shining talent, their strongest suit, their best quality. Wouldn't you be attracted to someone who paid you that highest compliment of acknowledgment? Of course you would. Now how do we do that?

"Repeat after me, 'I can see that you . . .'"

The brokers look puzzled. They were still digesting what Bob had told them.

"Come on. Let's hear it," Bob urged them, "repeat these words, 'I can see that you . . .'"

The brokers muttered the words.

"I can't hear you," yelled Bob. "Repeat these words, 'I can see that you . . . .'" He lent a cadence to the phrase.

Now they chimed in. Eight hundred and fifty brokers yelled back, "I can see that you . . . ." Then they laughed for they were slightly confused, not knowing where Bob was headed.

"Again," Bob shouted.

"I CAN SEE THAT YOU . . . ."

Bob laughed with them and waited till they settled down again.

"All you have to do now is fill in the blank.

'I CAN SEE THAT YOU *get done whatever you set your mind to*.'

'I CAN SEE THAT YOU *are great with people*.'

'I CAN SEE THAT YOU *enjoy following a job through to its completion*.'

'I CAN SEE THAT YOU *let nothing slip through the cracks*.'

"These are all acknowledgment statements reflecting each style.

"This is *connecting* with the person you're speaking with; it's what makes a business meeting a success. The person feels you know him or her. And you *do*, because you took the time to listen."

The brokers trusted what Bob said because he poured out a passion that came from deep inside. He had the credibility of one who has experienced everything he gave them.

A hand was raised in the back of the room. "Question?" Bob asked.

The broker stood up and said, "Bob, it's easy to acknowledge and connect with people when they're on their best behavior, but how do you connect with people who are showing their *ineffective* traits. If someone is being argumentative about the choice of stocks our company is recommending, how do I connect with him or her? What do I acknowledge?"

149

"What style is reflecting those traits?" asked Bob sitting on the stool he brought to the front of the stage.

"Dominance," said the broker.

"That's right. What are some of the *effective* traits of the Dominance style?"

The broker turned to her handout sheet and studied it for a moment. "Well, he seems to be direct and self-assured, and . . ."

"Stop right there," Bob said. "In your example you said he was complaining about your company's recommendations. Right?"

"Right," the broker responded.

"What's he *really* saying to you? That he is so self-assured he has his own way of doing things. That's why he's being argumentative. He has a better plan. To connect with him, acknowledge his assuredness; his extreme confidence in himself."

"Like . . ." said the broker.

"Like, 'I can see that you march to your own drummer. What are *your* stock choices?'"

"In other words," the broker interrupted, "put a positive spin on a negative trait."

"Yes. If a person is exhibiting ineffective traits, understand that on the other side of each negative trait is a positive trait."

Bob rose from the stool. "For example: a person with a Dominance style whose leadership is threatened could be dictatorial at your meeting; however, acknowledgment of his or her competitive nature will mitigate that negative behavior.

"When someone who displays the Influence style talks all the time to gain acceptance, the effective trait of being a people person is taken to an unhealthy extreme. If you acknowledge their people-person effective trait, what happens? They can relax, because they've been accepted by your acknowledgment.

"A person with the Steadiness style who is displaying a desire to keep the status quo to such an extent he or she won't budge, could easily be acknowledged. Simply say others look to him or her for calm in a storm. You've appealed to their higher calling. To overcome an ineffective trait acknowledge an effective trait.

"Someone displaying the Conscientiousness style can go overboard on gathering details and reach a point where he or she can't make decisions because of the need for one more detail. But if you acknowledge that person as one who lets nothing slip through the cracks, then he or she can lighten up. This requires some detective work on your part to read between the lines, but you can do it."

Then he put them to work. He read instructions from his workbook. He had them pair up with someone they didn't know and go through the process: Interview, Determine, Adapt, and Acknowledge. He was too busy to think about himself and the impact he was making. He was controlling the whole room: nurturing, cajoling, challenging them all as they practiced their interaction.

It was a thorough work-out session. As a finale, he had some brokers come up on stage and tell the audience their experience with each step of the process. Many admitted that this was the first time they *really* listened to someone. Others felt they could listen more easily because there was something specific (signposts) to listen for. Still others no longer feared silence in conversation. What Bob had done—what they had done for themselves—was prove the validity of the entire day's seminar. The results were astounding.

It was almost three o'clock when Bob picked up the stool and brought it down front. He took his time getting settled before he spoke.

"Any goal worth reaching takes time. It doesn't happen overnight. Let's face it, if you could achieve your goal in a single day, it wouldn't be much of a goal would it? The same applies to what we've covered today. It takes time to understand yourself, to deal with your strengths and weaknesses. It takes time to recognize personal styles of others. It takes time to learn to interview someone. It takes time to *hear* someone reveal their style traits. It takes time to adapt and acknowledge those traits. It takes time to connect. And over time, the benefits accrue as you help others celebrate their finest qualities; make them feel good in your presence.

"You are your highest priority; therefore, you are your own leader. And, my friends," he spoke slower, accenting each word, "leaders always know who they are!"

He let his hands fall into his lap and bowed his head. For a moment there was silence. Two seconds, three seconds. Then the room exploded with applause. Long, appreciative applause. They even stood. He raised his head and made eye-contact with every part of the room. That's when he saw Josh making his way down the aisle escorting a woman in military uniform. What was that all about . . . wait . . . that's Alex!

He jumped from the stage and the three of them hugged: Bob, Josh, and Marine Corporal Alexandra Crater. As the continuing applause washed over Bob, he beamed in triumph.

While Bob was not seeking acceptance, as he sought when he was a little boy, he received it. While he was not trying to please, he did. Yes, he was still making his living pleasing people. But it was different now. He was teaching others to be pleased with themselves, to focus on their marvelous traits, to reach out and connect with anyone . . . including—maybe even especially— themselves.

TWENTY-NINE

As the three of them sat at the dinner table, Bob thought how intricately connected they were to one person—Doc Crater. It was Doc's caring advice that triggered a series of life changing events for each of them.

For Bob, a new career; for Josh, a closer relationship with his daughter; for Alex, a new direction.

Alex said, "Bob, were you surprised when you saw Dad and me coming down the aisle at your seminar?"

"Surprised isn't the word for it. Listen," he said as he drew his chair closer to the table. "Moments before I saw you, I finished my seminar to silence; absolute silence. They didn't applaud! My heart sank. I didn't know what to think. Then, like a clap of thunder, they applauded. They were even *standing*! I looked around the room for the only person who knew how important this moment was for me. I looked for your Dad. When I saw him, I was confused. Who was that with him in uniform? Then I realized it was you!" Bob sighed and leaned back in his chair. "Well, it was just overwhelming."

Then Bob turned the conversation to Alex. "I haven't asked the most obvious question of the day. Alex? Why are you . . . ?"

"A Marine?" she finished his question with a giggle.

"I thought you were starting a career in real estate?"

"Oh, that lasted about ten minutes," she said laughing. "Then I worked as a waitress, then I helped out at a day-care center. Then . . ."

"Then I sat her down and we had a talk," said Josh with mock firmness.

"Alex?" said Bob. "You actually *listened* to your Dad?" He chuckled.

"Yeesss, I listened to the old codger." She leaned her head on her Dad's shoulder.

"What did you tell her, Josh?"

Josh leaned forward. "Bob, I asked if she

wanted to hear my perspective on the direction she was taking with her life."

"And you willingly accepted that, Alex?" asked Bob seriously.

"Well, I knew I needed some sort of direction, and we'd been having such great conversations. I figured maybe it *was* time for me to listen."

"What did he say?"

"He told me he thought I was afraid to make a commitment."

"Heavy observation."

"I'll say," said Alex.

Josh said, "Two days later she comes home with the news, she's joined the Marines."

"Can't make a bigger commitment than *Semper Fi*," said Alex emphatically. "But Bob, you know what I'm really sorry about? I'm sorry for the grief I caused Mom and Dad when I ran away from home. Guess you thought that was pretty stupid."

"Alex . . . you don't have to say anything about that."

"Well, it was a stupid thing to do."

Bob took a deep breath and said, "Let me tell you something about me. Years ago, when I was at an all boys school, I was having a hard time coping because the boys were making fun of my high voice and complete lack of whiskers. I was also flunking French; couldn't memorize the irregular verbs. So you know what I decided to do?"

"What?" said Alex leaning in.

"I decided to run away."

They both looked surprised.

"Did you?" asked Josh.

"Listen to how bright I was," Bob said. "The school was in farm country. Any farmer driving down the road would know that a fourteen year old in a blue suit holding a little suitcase in one hand and waving his thumb with the other was running away. The farmer who picked me up simply said, 'Son, you'll never forgive yourself.' He turned the truck around and headed back to the school. That's all he had to say.

"I guess what I'm saying, Alex, is we can never run away—literally or figuratively—from our highest priority, ourselves."

Josh and Alex both nodded as Bob took a sip of water and sat back in his chair.

"Bob," said Alex. "When I came back home during high school, Dad showed me the styles you drew up in Boston. Those are amazing. I believe they helped me become platoon leader, because I could understand what made some of the recruits tick. I want to thank you for that. But more than that," she said, reaching over to Josh, "I want to thank you for bringing us together." She gave her Dad a hug.

Josh, not usually given to displays of affection, hugged her tightly.

"Bob," said Josh, "I want to tell you about this Marine here."

Bob smiled and Alex raised an eyebrow in anticipation of what her Dad was going to say.

"Have you ever been to Parris Island?"

"No, I haven't," said Bob.

"Well, after the sentry lets you in, you drive along a curved road to the center of camp. Maybe it was seeing the young people in uniform or the statue of the flag raising on Iwo Jima that we passed, but the feelings Suzie and I felt were similar: patriotism, sacrifice, pride.

"We stood on a street corner, where the platoons would pass on their way to the graduation site, hoping to see Alex.

"Suzie says, 'Here come some women Marines.' We looked for Alex. I didn't see her right off. Suzie did. She whispered to me, 'There she is on the outside, fourth row back.' Well, I

159

couldn't believe my eyes. This one here," he nodded to Alex, "is marching ramrod straight and eyes ahead on her way to the huge tarmac. We followed them to their position in front of the bleachers. We took our seats with the other parents and guests."

Bob looked at Alex. Her eyes never left Josh. She enjoyed hearing her Dad replay her graduation.

"Suzie and I just couldn't believe it. Just sixteen weeks ago here was this unfocused, bratty . . ."

"Dad!" said Alex in mock indignation.

"Well you were, Alex. There's no other word for it. Now, let me finish. This bratty kid was now a disciplined, proud young woman." He stopped for a sip of water.

"That's me, Bob," whispered Alex. "I'm the proud young woman."

Bob smiled at both of them.

Josh continued. "Well, it's a good thing Suzie had some Kleenex with her because when the commanding officer said . . . 'Today you are a Marine. For as long as you live, you will always be a Marine.' Well, the tears started coming down Suzie's cheeks."

"Mom really cried?" asked Alex.

160

"She did, and I didn't do much better."

"Why?"

"Alex, let me put it this way. Number one, the reason I didn't cry was . . ."

Bob watched Alex stiffen. He burst out laughing. Josh maintained his serious gaze. Then Alex realized he was teasing her with his old 1-2-3 answer and she laughed, too, and gave her Dad a hug.

Josh looked over to Bob and they winked with fatherly understanding.

They had a wonderful evening together, and, when it was time for Josh and Alex to leave for the airport, they made a silent good-bye toast. Bob watched them walk away with their arms around each other. A waiter poured Bob a fresh cup of decaf.

Waiting for it to cool, he thought of the standing ovation the stock brokers had given him. He thought of Josh, who had the courage to ask for help and was rewarded with a renewed closeness to his daughter. He thought of Alex— what a complete surprise to see her. Josh hadn't given him a clue she'd be with him, or that her new career was in the military. What a fine woman she'd become.

Then his thoughts turned back to the day he received Blaylock's memo, and how it had upset him; how he sought solace by the Mississippi and met the stranger—the *perfect* stranger—who sat by his side, became his mentor, and changed his life. Was it providence? Some things you never know.

But one thing he did know: You can never fully express yourself, never truly explore the outer edges of your talents, until you know what holds you back and what propels you forward. Not until you know yourself can you ever hope to savor personal satisfaction. Not until you know yourself can you totally believe in yourself.

And in that defining moment when your search is over—when you finally *can* believe in yourself—a gush of new breath flows forth with an awakening *"ah-hah!"* and you know you have made . . .

THE GREAT CONNECTION.

STYLES OF THE CHARACTERS

A.J. Blaylock and Alexandra Crater

DOMINANCE

Effective Traits   **Ineffective Traits**

- Direct and Self-Assured
- Seizes Challenges
- Competitive
- Results Oriented
- Fearless in confrontation

- Boastful
- Dictatorial
- Blunt
- Argumentative
- Difficult listener

Bob Hathaway

INFLUENCE

Effective Traits   **Ineffective Traits**

- People Person (social)
- Enthusiastic
- Persuasive
- Communicator
- Optimistic
- Entertaining

- Avoids Confrontation to Maintain Acceptance
- Exaggerates
- Overly Enthusiastic
- Talks Too Much
- Difficulty With Focus

Doc Crater and John Pratt

S T E A D I N E S S

Effective Traits

- Great Listener
- Consistent
- Loyal / Supportive
- Patient
- Persistent

Ineffective Traits

- Highly Sensitive
- Passive
- Indecisive
- Resists Change
- Overly Tolerant

Tom Wilcox and Josh Crater

C O N S C I E N T I O U S N E S S

Effective Traits

- Critical Thinker
- Detail Oriented
- Tactful
- Precise / Accurate
- Problem Solver

Ineffective Traits

- Perfectionist
- Overly Critical
- Few Gray Areas
- Difficulty with Change
- Detached and Aloof

ABOUT THE AUTHOR

ARNIE WARREN'S VOICE is familiar across America as a radio and TV spokesperson. His career has taken him from top morning radio personality in Miami to CBS Radio and recognition by *Radio and Records* as one of the nation's best interviewers. *Fortune* 500 companies such as Chevrolet, Burger King, Citibank, and Motorola continue to call on him for their on-camera corporate presentations. Mr. Warren records books for the blind for The Library of Congress. His background as a University of Miami teacher serves him in the seminars he conducts in the U.S., Canada, and the Pacific Rim. Credentials as an educator, businessman, and broadcast entertainer have made him a frequent keynote speaker. He lives in Fort Lauderdale, Florida.

YOU ARE YOUR HIGHEST PRIORITY